Trends in Terrorism

Threats to the United States
and the Future of the
Terrorism Risk Insurance Act

Peter Chalk, Bruce Hoffman,
Robert Reville, Anna-Britt Kasupski

RAND CENTER FOR TERRORISM
RISK MANAGEMENT POLICY

The research described in this report was conducted by the RAND
Center for Terrorism Risk Management Policy.

Library of Congress Cataloging-in-Publication Data

Trends in terrorism : threats to the United States and the future of the Terrorism Risk
  Insurance Act / Peter Chalk ... [et al.].
    p. cm.
    "MG-393."
    Includes bibliographical references.
    ISBN 0-8330-3822-2 (pbk. : alk. paper)
    1. Terrorism—United States. 2. Terrorism insurance—United States. 3. United
States. Terrorism Risk Insurance Act of 2002. I. Chalk, Peter. II. Title.

HV6432.T75 2005
303.6'25'0973—dc22

2005018552

The RAND Corporation is a nonprofit research organization providing
objective analysis and effective solutions that address the challenges
facing the public and private sectors around the world. RAND's
publications do not necessarily reflect the opinions of its research clients
and sponsors.

RAND® is a registered trademark.

Published 2005 by the RAND Corporation
1776 Main Street, P.O. Box 2138, Santa Monica, CA 90407-2138
1200 South Hayes Street, Arlington, VA 22202-5050
201 North Craig Street, Suite 202, Pittsburgh, PA 15213-1516
RAND URL: http://www.rand.org/
To order RAND documents or to obtain additional information, contact
Distribution Services: Telephone: (310) 451-7002;
Fax: (310) 451-6915; Email: order@rand.org

The RAND Center for Terrorism Risk Management Policy (CTRMP)

CTRMP provides research that is needed to inform public and private decisionmakers on economic security in the face of the threat of terrorism. Terrorism risk insurance studies provide the backbone of data and analysis to inform appropriate choices with respect to the renewal of the Terrorism Risk Insurance Act of 2002 (TRIA) in 2005. Research on the economics of various liability decisions informs the policy decisions of the U.S. Congress and the opinions of state and federal judges. Studies of compensation help Congress to ensure that appropriate compensation is made to the victims of terrorist attacks. Research on security helps to protect critical infrastructure and to improve collective security in rational and cost-effective ways.

CTRMP is housed at the RAND Corporation, an international nonprofit research organization with a reputation for rigorous and objective analysis and the world's leading provider of research on terrorism. The center combines three organizations:

- RAND Institute for Civil Justice, which brings a 25-year history of empirical research on liability and compensation.
- RAND Infrastructure, Safety, and Environment, which conducts research on homeland security and public safety.
- Risk Management Solutions, the world's leading provider of models and services for catastrophe risk management.

For additional information about the Center for Terrorism Risk Management Policy, contact:

Robert Reville
RAND Corporation
1776 Main Street
P.O. Box 2138
Santa Monica, CA 90407
Robert_Reville@rand.org
(310) 393-0411, Ext. 6786

Debra Knopman
RAND Corporation
1200 South Hayes Street
Arlington, VA 22202
Debra_Knopman@rand.org
(703) 413-1100, Ext. 5667

A profile of the CTRMP, abstracts of its publications, and ordering information can be found on at http://www.rand.org/multi/ctrmp/.

Center for Terrorism Risk Management Policy Advisory Board

Preface

Following the 9/11 terrorist attacks, concerns about the insurance industry's ability to provide coverage against the risk of terrorism led Congress to pass TRIA. The act requires insurers to offer commercial insurance that will pay on claims that occur from a terrorist attack, and for losses on the scale of 9/11, TRIA provides a "backstop" in the form of free reinsurance. TRIA's impending "sunset"—on December 31, 2005—presents the opportunity to examine whether the structure and style of government involvement, and the terrorism insurance market that it has created, provide appropriate financial protection against the current threat of terrorism. In other words, how does the architecture of TRIA align with the underlying terrorism risk?

This book examines current and future trends in terrorism. The focus of the analysis is on developments that have relevance for terrorist attacks taking place within the borders of the continental United States and the extent to which they are addressed (or not) by the TRIA framework. This book should be of interest to federal and state policymakers, insurers, commercial policyholders, and others who have a stake in ensuring the economic security of the United States in the face of the terrorist threat.

This is one of a series of reports that the RAND Center for Terrorism Risk Management Policy is planning to publish to inform policymakers on terrorism insurance, compensation, and liability. The CTRMP is funded through pooled contributions from corporations, foundations, and trade organizations.

Contents

Summary

Introduction

The Terrorism Risk Insurance Act of 2002 (TRIA) was crafted in the aftermath of the 9/11 attacks after the insurance industry, stung by $32 billion in damage claims (by current estimates) and fearing another attack of equal magnitude, began to exclude terrorism coverage from policies. The legislation requires insurance companies to make terrorism insurance available to customers and, in return, provides federal reinsurance (a "backstop") for losses from terrorist attacks. It is intended to give insurers time to assess their exposure to terrorism risk and to consider how to price and underwrite the risk. TRIA is set to expire at the end of December 2005.

TRIA embodies federal policy that a private insurance market will provide the foundation of the financial recovery from future terrorist attacks. It also recognizes that since the risk is unfamiliar to the industry, federal government assistance should, at least in the short run, be made available to support this market.

In this book, we examine whether this policy and, in particular, the architecture of TRIA provide robust protection against the threat of losses from future attacks. By robust, we ask specifically whether the structure of TRIA is in line with the fundamental qualities of the risk of terrorism and with likely evolving trends in this threat. The focus of the analysis is on developments that have relevance for terrorist attacks taking place within the borders of the continental United States and the extent to which they are addressed (or not) by the TRIA framework.

What Is The Evolving Threat?

Al Qaeda clearly represents the principal focus of current U.S. concern about transnational terrorism. The network has not only explicitly defined its ideological and operational agenda as one directed against American citizens and property, it has also demonstrated a proven capability to effectively employ land, air, and sea modalities against target venues that have ranged from hotels to state-of-the-art warships. Nothing suggests that the group's hardcore leadership has changed its views since December 2003, when bin Laden vowed to pursue Americans "in their own backyard."

That said, it is evident that the character of al Qaeda today differs markedly from what it was when it organized and executed the suicide attacks of September 11, 2001. The loss of its safe haven in Afghanistan, combined with the capture and/or elimination of many of its critical field commanders and functionaries, has forced the group to reconfigure its operational agenda—away from centrally controlled strategic assaults executed by an inner core of jihadist activists and toward tactically oriented strikes undertaken by affiliated cells (and sometimes individuals) as and when opportunities arise. In many ways, the largely monolithic structure that emerged out of Afghanistan in the late 1990s now better correlates to an amorphous "movement of movements" that is more nebulous, segmented, and polycentric in character.

Based on these developments, one can postulate four trends that are likely to become manifest, all of which have relevance for threat contingencies in the United States:

- A continuing interest in attacking hard targets, but an increased focus on soft, civilian-centric venues.
- An ongoing emphasis on economic attacks.
- Continued reliance on suicide strikes.
- A desire to use chemical, biological, radiological, and nuclear (CBRN) weapons but little ability to execute large-scale unconventional attacks.

In addition to the terrorist threats posed by al Qaeda and both associated and independent radical jihadists, a growing groundswell of domestically inspired radicalism has emerged that appears to be based on the spreading phenomenon of anti-globalization (AG). The AG movement has had an impact on at least three homegrown entities—all of which have demonstrated, in varying degrees, an explicit penchant for violence and civilian-directed action:

- Anarchists, who resonate with the claim that international trade and commerce are, in fact, a mask designed to hide and covertly advance U.S. global economic, cultural, and political power.
- Far-right extremists, who reject the loss of individual identity associated with international movements of people, commodities, and money; who oppose the concentration of power that globalization entails; and who argue that globalization is an American-led conspiracy conducted by and for the benefit of Jewish capitalists.
- Radical environmentalists, who now routinely denigrate corporate power and capitalism (and the unrestrained discretionary spending that they entail) as posing the single greatest threat to the planet and its life.

A notable common thread in many of the trends is an increased risk for the private sector. This increase arises from the changes in the operational environment because of the Global War on Terror; the hardening of government facilities, which is shifting risk to softer targets; the rise of extremists motivated by AG and therefore hostile to corporate power; and the increased focus by al Qaeda on attacks that yield magnified economic consequences. These changes raise the stakes for ensuring a properly functioning insurance system that protects against these risks.

Does TRIA Provide Robust Protection Against These Threats?

The results of our comparison of these trends in the underlying risk to the architecture of TRIA and the insurance market shaped by it has led to two primary conclusions:

- *TRIA does not provide adequate financial protection, particularly in the face of economically motivated attacks.* Specifically, take-up rates for terrorism insurance may be too low, thus escalating the risk of disruption after future attacks and undermining resilience. As al Qaeda increasingly advertises its interest in attacks with magnified economic consequences, and as the private sector becomes more the concerted focus of terrorist attacks, a growing necessity has emerged to fortify the institutions that buffer the economic consequences of such an attack. Insurance provides funds to compensate injured victims and the families of the deceased, sustain business operations during disruption, and rebuild damaged and destroyed assets and infrastructure. However, take-up rates at current low levels (approximately 50 percent) are likely to lead to widespread uninsured losses, which would slow recovery and magnify the economic consequences.
- *TRIA has significant gaps and is not robust to an evolving threat.* Given contemporary trends in terrorism and the current architecture of TRIA, there remains a real possibility of large uninsured losses accruing in the near-to-medium term, which will significantly impede the recovery from some future attacks. The most profound risk occurs in the area of CBRN attacks, for which insurers are not required to offer coverage (except under workers' compensation). As a result, such attacks are typically excluded from most insurance policies. Another significant gap is the exclusion of domestic attacks; while such attacks are less of a risk than imported threats, they remain real and increasingly appear to be focusing on private-sector targets. The exclusion of domestic attacks is also problematic given the increased "fran-

chising" of terrorist attacks by al Qaeda to local affiliates and the added difficulty of attributing attacks to a particular group.

Policy Recommendations

Given these conclusions, this book emphasizes the following two suggestions:

- *Instead of allowing TRIA to sunset, particularly in the face of economically motivated terrorist attacks, Congress might prefer to consider policy measures that increase the take-up of terrorism insurance and lower its price.* These measures might include offering subsidies for the purchase of terrorism insurance or providing more risk sharing within the insurance industry in the form of lower TRIA "deductibles" for insurance companies. With lower individual company deductibles, if the entire industry's backstop remains the same (the industry "retention" of $15 billion), the price of terrorism insurance is likely to fall without increasing costs to taxpayers.
- *A long-term solution to providing terrorism insurance in the United States must address CBRN attacks and attacks by domestic groups.* While the extension of TRIA to domestic attacks is straightforward, extension to cover CBRN attacks poses significant challenges for insurance and may be appropriately covered through a direct government program.

Other suggestions include

- considering mandatory requirements for companies that own or operate systems vital to the functioning of U.S. critical infrastructure to carry adequate levels of insurance
- conducting further research on the ability of insurance to prompt increased security in the private sector

- establishing an oversight board to review TRIA or its successor's performance and ensure that it is robust to changes in the underlying risk.

Acknowledgments

We are grateful for the highly useful feedback from those who commented on earlier drafts of this book and helped to refine the analysis contained therein: Rohan Gunaratna of the Institute for Defense and Strategic Studies in Singapore; David Brannan, Adjunct Professor with the Monterey Naval Postgraduate School; Erwann Michel-Kerjan of the University of Pennsylvania; and Jack Riley of the RAND Corporation. We also thank Debra Knopman, Mike Wermuth, Lloyd Dixon, and Fred Kipperman of RAND for comments and advice. In addition, a special word of thanks is due to CTRMP for its generous support, advice, and assistance in facilitating the completion of this study. From the CTRMP Board, we particularly acknowledge Hemant Shah, the CEO of Risk Management Solutions, for suggesting the project. Finally, we thank Lisa Sheldone of the RAND Corporation for her tireless work in expediting and ensuring thorough quality assurance of the document, Paul Steinberg for his assistance with communications, and Christina Pitcher for her patient and excellent editorial assistance. Needless to say, any errors and omissions in the book are the sole responsibility of the authors.

CHAPTER ONE

Introduction

Background

The coordinated terrorist strikes of September 11, 2001, have led to an enormous response by the U.S. government to increase both physical and, to a lesser extent, financial security in the face of potential future attacks. With regard to physical security, an unprecedented Global War on Terrorism (GWOT) has been set in motion that has been instrumental in destroying al Qaeda's territorial base in the Taliban-controlled areas of Afghanistan; overthrowing the Hussein regime in Iraq; collapsing entrenched extremist Islamist cells from Hamburg to Singapore; galvanizing a major reassessment of American intelligence capabilities; and triggering, in the creation of the Department of Homeland Security, what is arguably the most ambitious attempt to overhaul the federal government since World War II. Now, more than at any other time in the past, terrorism has assumed a central place of importance in American foreign and domestic policy.

The most prominent federal measure to increase financial security was the passage of the Terrorism Risk Insurance Act (TRIA) in 2002, which was intended to stabilize insurance markets reeling from the enormity of claims made in relation to 9/11 losses. In response to the size of ensuing payouts from the attacks (the largest from a single event in history) and concerned that they could not adequately forecast or price terrorist risk and that they would not be able to cover additional strikes on the scale of the 9/11 attacks, many primary insurers and reinsurers[1] moved to limit or exclude terrorism coverage from their policies (see Dixon and Stern, 2004; Kunreuther and Michel-Kerjan, 2004b; Doherty, Lamm-Tennant, and Starks, 2003; and Chen, 2004).[2] The result was that terrorism insurance became either very expensive[3] or unavailable, generating concern within the wider business community that the lack of coverage would slow property and commercial development, impede the recovery from recession, and undermine the general ability of the country to recover from future attacks (Oxley, 2004; and U.S. GAO, 2004, introduction).[4]

TRIA requires insurance companies to make terrorism risk coverage available to all customers and, in return, guarantees that the government will provide federal reinsurance (a "backstop") for any losses above a certain amount. The act only covers attacks connected to "foreign" interests and, while not excluding chemical, biological, radiological, and nuclear (CBRN) attacks, does not specifically obligate insurers to offer this coverage.[5] In broad terms, TRIA encourages

---

[1] Reinsurers provide insurance to insurance companies, allowing insurance companies to spread their risks better.

[2] In December 2004, a federal jury ruled that the strikes on the World Trade Center constituted two separate attacks, entitling the building's developer, Larry Silverstein, to collect up to $2.2 billion; this is more than double the coverage provided by nine insurers at the complex. See Bagli, 2004.

[3] Premium rate increases following the 9/11 attacks rose, on average, between 10 and 50 percent. See "P/C Terrorism Insurance Coverage," 2004, p. 1; and "A Limitless Risk," 2002.

[4] The losses from 9/11 for insurance companies were, of course, in the form of payments to businesses and individuals affected by the attacks. Including government compensation and charity as well as insurance, the families of the deceased victims, the injured and ill surviving victims, businesses, unemployed workers, the City of New York, and others affected by the attacks received over $40 billion. These resources were used to pay for rebuilding structures, businesses, and individual lives and were no doubt critical to the recovery of the city and the country. The largest share of these resources, more than half, was paid by insurance companies. In this sense, the availability of insurance to pay terrorism losses may have been the most critical part of the financial security for New Yorkers during 9/11.

[5] CBRN exclusions may be disallowed by state regulators, and coverage may follow in some cases from other requirements, such as the inability to write exclusions on workers' compensation.

an insurance market that covers terrorist attacks perpetrated by foreign groups that involve the use of conventional weapons, including catastrophic attacks on the scale of 9/11 and larger.

When the legislation was passed, TRIA was intended to give insurers time to assess their exposure to terrorism risk and to consider how to price and underwrite the risk. TRIA is set to expire at the end of December 2005.

Objective

This book is intended to review the contemporary terrorist threat to the continental United States as a means of informing decisions about the termination, renewal, or reconceptualization of TRIA. While a literature on the economics of terrorism insurance is developing (Smetters, 2004; Kunreuther and Michel-Kerjan, 2004b; Lakdawalla and Zanjani, forthcoming), this book takes the approach of starting with the underlying risk of terrorism and only then asking whether the policy of government involvement—and the insurance market encouraged thereby—is suited to the threat environment as it appears to be evolving. Specifically, we seek to answer the question, Does the market for terrorism insurance encouraged by TRIA provide financial security that aligns with the evolving terrorism threat?

Organization of This Book

In the next chapter, we provide a brief overview of the architecture of TRIA and of the terrorism insurance market since the 9/11 attacks. Then, in the next two chapters, we describe the trends with respect to the dominant terrorist threat—al Qaeda and other foreign threats—and the trends with respect to the threat of terrorist attacks from domestic groups. In each chapter, after reviewing the trends, we describe the implications for terrorism insurance public policy. In the final chapter, we conclude with lessons learned for the renewal of TRIA and with policy recommendations.

CHAPTER TWO

The Architecture of TRIA and an Overview of Terrorism Insurance Since 9/11

As noted above, TRIA was intended to provide federal support and encouragement for the development of a private terrorism commercial insurance market following the 9/11 attacks.[1] The legislation requires insurance companies to make certain kinds of terrorism risk coverage available to customers and, in return, provides federal reinsurance (a "backstop") for any losses thereby incurred. The government does not receive any premium for providing this reinsurance, meaning that it is effectively free. To be eligible for Treasury reinsurance, acts of terrorism must be "certified," meaning they have to be both committed by a *foreign* interest and result in property and casualty damage of at least $5 million. Certified losses are capped at $100 billion under the authorization of the Terrorism Risk Insurance Program (which is administered by the Treasury), with those losses exceeding this limit subject to congressional discretion (U.S. Congress, 2002, sections 102 and 103; "A Limitless Risk," 2002; Kun-

---

[1] Section 101(b) of the act (U.S. Congress, 2002) states that it is intended to

> establish a temporary Federal program that provides for a transparent system of shared public and private compensation for insured losses resulting from acts of terrorism, in order to—1. protect consumers by addressing market disruptions and ensure the continued widespread availability and affordability of property and casualty insurance for terrorism risk; and 2. allow for a transitional period for the private markets to stabilize, resume pricing of such insurance, and build capacity to absorb any future losses, while preserving State insurance regulation and consumer protections.

reuther and Michel-Kerjan, 2004b, p. 204). The program is set to sunset on December 31, 2005.[2]

The TRIA mechanism stipulates that primary insurers are responsible for a deductible, which they must pay in advance of any federal reinsurance. In 2005, this figure was calculated as 15 percent of a group's direct earned premiums on commercial property and casualty policies during the previous year. In effect, for large insurance groups, this deductible can be quite high—well over $1 billion. Once an insurer has met its deductible, the Department of the Treasury covers 90 percent of its losses, with the insurer paying the remaining 10 percent.

For attacks with insured losses below $15 billion, TRIA primarily serves as a provider of liquidity and as a risk-sharing mechanism for the insurance industry, with no expected payment from the Treasury to those who are insured. This is because while the federal government will cover the losses of a particular firm that has met its deductible, the program is obligated to recover the payments through a surcharge on policies in subsequent years. Repayment is also possible for losses above $15 billion, although it is optional. Thus, in effect, the program is intended to absorb the risk to the industry for attacks only of comparable size to 9/11 and larger. (For a detailed description, see forthcoming RAND research by Stephen Carroll, Tom LaTourrette, and Craig Martin on losses and compensation for terrorist attacks).

TRIA applies only to certain lines of commercial insurance, of which the most prominent are commercial property, business interruption, workers' compensation, and general liability. Except for general liability, these were among the lines most affected by the attacks

---

[2] TRIA represents a policy decision that the private sector should cover the losses that it experiences from terrorist attacks. An alternative proposal considered initially after 9/11, as noted by Paul O'Neill, secretary of the Treasury on 9/11, was public compensation for terrorism losses. The reason for limiting the federal role, according to O'Neill, is to avoid providing incentives to under-invest in security, and because the insurance industry has experience and infrastructure for pricing risks and processing claims. This decision, however, significantly shapes the relative public-private responsibilities for protection and for covering losses (U.S. Department of the Treasury, 2001).

of 9/11 (Dixon and Stern, 2004; Hartwig, 2004), reflecting the intent of the legislation to cover attacks like the one that had just occurred. The act does not apply to homeowners or auto coverage, which are referred to as "personal lines coverage, or to life insurance, which experienced significant losses on 9/11.

The reinsurance under TRIA applies to CBRN attacks if the insurance policy covers attacks involving these weapons. However, the act does not require that insurers offer this coverage, and insurers have been excluding this coverage from most policies (Marsh Inc., 2004, pp. 34–35).

As noted, TRIA is set to sunset at the end of 2005. There are at least two reasons why the program may have been developed and enacted according to this limited timeframe: Either the threat of terrorism was considered temporary or the market's inability to provide coverage at affordable rates was deemed temporary. The first possibility has clearly proven false. Not only has the threat of terrorism clearly outlasted TRIA, the Bush administration has repeatedly affirmed that the struggle against extremism and fanaticism is one that will necessarily have to be fought over the long haul.

More likely, TRIA's duration reflects government thinking that the turmoil in the terrorism insurance market was a temporary aberration brought about 9/11 and one that would be corrected relatively quickly. Empirically, there is some evidence for this contention. During the first nine months of 2002, for instance, rates for property coverage declined by an average of between 50 to 75 percent and since 2003 have continued to fall by roughly one-half. In the third quarter of 2004, the typical price for terrorism insurance represented around 4 percent of the total premium for property coverage, compared to 10 percent in the third quarter of 2003 (Congressional Budget Office, 2005; Shadow Financial Regulatory Committee, 2002; and Jeffrey Brown et al., 2004). That said, these price changes have occurred only with the act's backstop in place. How much price or availability will change if this safety net is removed is somewhat difficult to discern. However, without the guarantee of federal terrorism reinsurance, terrorism insurance rates will likely rise once again.

It is not surprising that as prices have fallen, the fraction of companies that purchase terrorism coverage (or "take-up rates") have increased. One study undertaken by Marsh Inc. in 2004, for instance, showed that 44 percent of large companies bought terrorism coverage in the third quarter of 2004, compared with only 26 percent for the same period the previous year. Another survey by Aon produced figures of 57 percent (2004) versus 24 percent (2003). The take-up rates vary somewhat depending on the region and industry, with higher take-up rates in the Eastern and Midwestern United States (58 percent and 60 percent, respectively, according to Marsh) than in the South and West (29 and 38 percent, respectively) (Congressional Budget Office, 2005, pp. 6–7; Marsh Inc., 2004; and Aon Corporation, 2004).

Again, interpreting and assessing the significance of these figures is extremely difficult. While terrorism insurance take-up rates are equal to or higher than those for other catastrophic risks, such as hurricanes and earthquakes,[3] this could reflect a failure of these markets as well. From a public policy perspective, the question is more appropriately whether these take-up rates will provide resilience in the face of future attacks and whether the losses of a future attack are spread across those at risk. By this standard, compared to the 100 percent take-up rate by default on the day of the 9/11 attacks, take-up rates of 57 percent are very low. If TRIA is allowed to sunset, given the likely increase in prices, and assuming no change in the perception of risk by those who are insured, it is likely that take-up rates will fall.

An aspect of TRIA that has stimulated some controversy is the effect of TRIA on private-sector incentives to adopt security and other loss-mitigation measures. It is possible that the provision of free reinsurance has reduced the incentive to adopt protective measures

---

[3] The take-up rate for earthquake insurance in California is 17 percent (Jaffee, and Russell, 2000). The take-up rate for flood coverage in flood-prone areas is about 50 percent. Coverage is roughly twice as high in the mandatory part of the market (flood insurance is required on properties with a loan issued by a federally regulated lender) than for homes where flood insurance is not required. Therefore, take-up rates when flood insurance is not required are low—on the order of one-third (Lloyd Dixon, Noreen Clancy, and Seth Seabury, unpublished RAND research on the market penetration rate for flood insurance).

(Congressional Budget Office (2005). Some progress has been made in developing quantitative terrorism risk models that can inform risk-based pricing (Kunreuther, Michel-Kerjan, and Porter, 2005; Congressional Budget Office, 2005, p. 4), which would encourage companies seeking insurance to invest in security measures to receive lower insurance rates. However, there is no evidence that insurance companies are using these models for pricing. The issue of mitigation and insurance has excited controversy because both those who are insured and insurers have argued that there is little information with which to evaluate the effectiveness of private security measures, and for many types of attacks, it is unclear what measures can be taken. Also, the U.S. Department of Homeland Security reportedly is interested in encouraging the adoption of private security measures through insurance pricing (Savage, 2005). At the same time, if take-up rates drop as a result of increased pricing after the removal of free reinsurance, the ability to encourage security measures through insurance pricing will be limited.

In summary, TRIA has largely encouraged a market for terrorism insurance that, as long as the provision of free federal reinsurance continues, can be expected to cover contingencies on a par with those that occurred on 9/11 (that is, attacks carried out with conventional weapons, perpetrated by foreign terrorist groups, and directed against commercial assets). By the same token, if the act is allowed to sunset, it is reasonable to conclude that resulting price increases and reduced take-up rates will work to limit the role of commercial insurance in offsetting the losses and costs associated with future attacks taking place on American soil.[4]

---

[4] It is important to note that other means of corporate financial risk management for terrorism, such as catastrophe bonds, may emerge if commercial insurance declines with the sunset of TRIA. See, for instance, Smetters, 2004 and discussion in Dixon et al., 2004.

CHAPTER THREE

Al Qaeda and Imported Terrorist Threats to the United States Post-9/11

The first step toward assessing whether TRIA is aligned with the risk of terrorism today is to examine the nature, scope, and tempo of imported threats emanating from al Qaeda—the main focus of U.S. concern with regard to transnational militant extremism.[1] In this chapter, we discuss the evolving threat from al Qaeda and include a discussion of implications for terrorism insurance public policy.

What Is the Context for the Evolving Threat?

The al Qaeda network has not only explicitly defined its ideological and operational agenda as one directed against American citizens and property,[2] it has also demonstrated a proven capability to effectively

---

[1] Several other groups pose threats to areas of U.S. strategic interest, including Basque Fatherland and Freedom (ETA), Hezbollah, the Moro Islamic Liberation Front, the New People's Army, and the Revolutionary Armed Forces of Colombia (FARC). Although a number of these organizations have a potential global reach—notably, Hezbollah, FARC, and ETA—for the most part, they have largely limited their operational activities to local targets. Moreover, other than ad hoc, pragmatic, tactical linkages, they have not (yet) moved to forge a truly transnational network of operational cadres. This has clearly not been the case with al Qaeda, which has shown both a willingness and capability to act on a concerted international scale, drawing on affiliates from London to Bali.

[2] Arguably, the clearest expression of this intent came with the 1998 Khost *fatwa*, which explicitly affirmed killing Americans—wherever and whenever it was possible—as an individual duty that all Muslims were required to observe and fulfill. See "Text of the World Islamic Front's Statement," 1998. For an interesting analysis of the 1998 *fatwa* see Ranstorp, 1998, pp. 321–327.

employ land, air, and sea modalities against target venues that have ranged from hotels to state-of-the-art warships. More pointedly, al Qaeda has repeatedly affirmed its ongoing intention to attack facilities directly on U.S. soil and, at the time of this writing, had apparently been linked to a series of planned assaults on major financial institutions in Washington, D.C., New Jersey, and New York City (Peterson and Meyer, 2004). Nothing suggests that the group's hardcore leadership has changed its views since December 2003, when bin Laden vowed to pursue Americans "in their own backyard" ("Al-Jazirah Airs," 2003). As former Director of Central Intelligence George J. Tenet testified before Congress in February 2004 (Tenet, 2004):

> [Al Qaeda] detainees consistently talk about the importance the group still attaches to striking the main enemy: the United States. Across the operational spectrum—air, maritime, special weapons—we have time and time again uncovered plots that are chilling.

That said, it is evident that the character of al Qaeda today differs markedly from that which organized and executed the suicide attacks of September 11, 2001. Benefiting from access to secure territorial basing in Taliban-controlled areas of Afghanistan, the movement had taken on many traits of a hierarchical organization by the late 1990s, complete with permanent installations, fixed structures, standardized methods, and regular procedures.[3] Most terrorism analysts generally agree that it was these factors that enabled long-term planning and training for the perpetration of high-profile strategic attacks, such as those that were witnessed in Kenya and Tanzania in 1998[4] and New York and Washington, D.C., three years later.[5]

---

[3] For an excellent overview of this period, see Rashid, 2000, chapter 10.

[4] The attacks in Kenya and Tanzania—which were against the U.S. embassies in Nairobi and Dar es Salaam—are generally considered to be the first concerted demonstration of al Qaeda's intent to act on the Khost *fatwa* by targeting prominent symbols of American political, military, and diplomatic power. The near simultaneous bombings resulted in 391 deaths (291 in Kenya and 10 in Tanzania) and more than 5,000 casualties. See Office of the Coordinator for Counterterrorism, 1999, p. 3.

However, the ferocity of 9/11 unleashed a U.S. response that was not only equally as dramatic in its dimensions but that has also decisively limited the environmental and strategic context in which al Qaeda is able to operate. Within a month of the 9/11 attacks, a full-scale military assault on the Taliban regime in Afghanistan had commenced (Operation Enduring Freedom), toppling the regime of Mullah Omar and scattering the core of al Qaeda's leadership to various locales in the Middle East and throughout Central, South, and Southeast Asia (Huband, Alden, and Fidler, 2003). A subsequent and unremitting campaign of harassment and intelligence tracking has resulted in the capture or elimination of many of these central commanders, which as of May 2005 included, among others,

- Ramzi bin al-Shibi (the reputed recruiter for the 9/11 attacks) ("News Conference Regarding Zacarias Moussaoui," 2001)
- Mohammed Atef, Abu Zubaydah, and Khaled Sheikh Mohammad (all senior operational planners) (Van Natta, 2003; Finn, 2002; Eccleston, 2003; FBI, 2005; and "A Timely Arrest," 2003)
- Abd al-Rahim al-Nashirih (bin Laden's alleged point man on the Arabian Peninsula and chief organizer for maritime attacks such as the USS Cole suicide strike in 2000) (Shenon, 2002)
- Riduan Isamuddin (also known as Hambali, al Qaeda's main link to Southeast Asian militant groups and the accused mastermind of the 2002 Bali attacks in Indonesia) ("Key Asian," 2003)
- Ahmed Khalfan Ghilani (one of the FBI's 22 most wanted terrorists and believed to be a key figure behind the 1998 U.S. embassy attacks in Kenya and Tanzania) (Johnson and Diamond, 2004)

---

[5] See, for example, Gunaratna, 2002, p. 73. Certain observers go further, arguing that Operation Enduring Freedom actually destroyed al Qaeda's structural coherence. According to Burke (2003), for instance, "the nearest thing to al-Qaeda, as popularly understood, existed for a short period, between 1996 and 2001. Its base had been Afghanistan and what I had seen in Tora Bora were the final scenes of its destruction."

- Abu Faraj al-Libbi (thought to be al Qaeda's third most senior leader in 2005 and main coordinator for operations in Pakistan) (Masood and Khan, 2005)
- Haitham al-Yemeni (described as a central figure in facilitating the international dissemination of jihadist communications and supplies) (Jehl, 2005).

On the monetary front, al Qaeda has also suffered somewhat. Thus far, over $136 million[6] in identifiable assets have been seized or frozen, potentially representing the equivalent of two to two and half years of operating funds (Huband, Alden, and Fidler, 2003).[7] Of greater significance, the heightened imperative attached to decisively cutting the international flow of terrorist finances has forced al Qaeda to progressively adapt its jihadist "business model" and switch to more secure, but less lucrative localized collection methods. The resulting drop in revenue has compounded the strategic setbacks noted above, further denuding the group of the necessary resource inputs to plan and execute large-scale, complex attacks on the scale of 9/11 (Kiser, 2005). Remarking on the general utility of this aspect of the GWOT, David Aufhauser, the former general counsel for the U.S. Treasury, observes: "Starving them [al Qaeda] of money really has a dramatic impact on the license and liberty with which they previously roamed the world" (David Aufhauser, cited in Huband, Alden, and Fidler, 2003).

These various developments have had a marked effect on al Qaeda's institutional makeup, which during the course of the past three years has become progressively more fluid and decentralized. Specifically, the loss of a secure haven in Afghanistan and the loss of key human and capital resources have stripped the group of the vital

---

[6] Of this amount, $36 million has been confiscated by the United States and $100 million by the international community. It should be noted, however, that the former figure includes assets seized under the Clinton administration, while much of the latter has been unfrozen because of lack of concrete evidence that these monies were being used to support terrorism.

[7] This approximation is based on estimates that during its heyday, al Qaeda enjoyed an annual operating budget of between $30 million and $50 million.

command, logistical, and functional assets needed to operate in a vertically organized manner. Accordingly, al Qaeda has been increasingly
forced to reconfigure its operational agenda—away from centrally
controlled strategic assaults executed by an inner core of jihadist activists and toward tactically oriented strikes undertaken by affiliated
cells (and sometimes individuals) as and when opportunities arise. In
many ways, the largely monolithic structure that emerged out of Afghanistan in the late 1990s now better correlates to an amorphous
"movement of movements" that while undoubtedly motivated by the
continuing message of transnational jihadism—itself strengthened by
the GWOT—is more nebulous, segmented, and polycentric in character (comments made during "New Trends in Terrorism," 2002; see
also Gunaratna, 2004, pp. 51–55; and "The Other War," 2003).
Commenting on this evolutionary dynamic, various analysts argue
that the GWOT, far from destroying bin Laden's movement, has actually given rise to a new, less predictable organization composed of
dozens of like-minded extremists, many of whom have willingly taken
up the Saudi renegade's call for global jihad independent of either his
money or training ("Al Qaeda: Organization or Ideology?" 2003; see
also Kenney, 2003).

Given This Context, What Does It Suggest for the Nature of Future Attacks?

One can postulate four trends that are likely to become manifest, all
of which have relevance for terrorist attacks in the United States:

- a continuing interest in attacking hard targets, but an increased
  focus on soft, civilian-centric venues
- an ongoing emphasis on economic attacks
- continued reliance on suicide strikes
- a desire to use CBRN weapons, but little ability to execute large-
  scale unconventional attacks.

Each of these is briefly discussed below. For each trend, we review the implications for public policy about financial risks to the private sector and, specifically, policy about TRIA.

A Continuing Interest in Hard Targets, but an Increased Focus on Soft, Civilian-Centric Venues

Despite the setbacks outlined above, al Qaeda will retain an active interest in attacking "hard"—that is, well protected—targets, such as embassies and military installations. These venues are not only symbolic of the strength and influence of bin Laden's self-defined enemies, they often represent the most difficult to penetrate. By striking out and destroying such facilities, al Qaeda underscores its credentials as a meaningful force, establishing a benchmark of power that can then be used to build morale and attract new recruits. Consider attacks against the American-led Coalition headquarters in Baghdad (2003); the United Nations compound, again in the Iraqi capital (2003) (McDonnell, 2004; Williams, 2004; and Farley, 2003); the central office of the Saudi General Security Service (the Kingdom's domestic intelligence agency) in Riyadh (2004) (MacFarquhar, 2004); and the U.S. consulates in Karachi and Jedda (2002 and 2004, respectively) ("Suicide Attack," 2002; and Bodi, 2004). Such attacks are indicative of the continued salience that hard targets hold for bin Laden and his cohorts.

Facilitating al Qaeda's ability to act against high-profile, well-protected facilities is the ongoing presence of Egyptian Islamic Jihad fighters within the group. Brought into bin Laden's movement by Ayman al-Zawahiri in 1998,[8] this nucleus of highly motivated militants constitutes the most educated, skilled, and competent cadre in the transnational jihadist movement. Critically, many of these jihadists have yet to be detained, continuing to play a pivotal role in

---

[8] Ayman al-Zawahiri is commonly postulated as the "brains" behind al Qaeda. He first met bin Laden in Afghanistan, then befriended the Saudi renegade in Sudan during 1993 when the global jihadist movement was still in its formative stages. In 1998 Zawahiri cosigned the Khost *fatwa*, an action that effectively tied his group (the Egyptian Islamic Jihad) to al Qaeda and its self-defined war against the United States and its Western/secular allies. For further details see Bergen, 2002, pp. 200–205; Wright, 2002, p. 83; and Miller, 2001.

solidifying the competence and determination of the remaining al Qaeda leadership. Just as significantly, they appear to be a key contributing factor behind the planning and mechanics for some of the group's more adventurous post-9/11 attacks (see Bruce Hoffman, 2003, p. 8; and "Al-Qaeda: Organization or Ideology?" 2003).

That said, al Qaeda's functional latitude for successfully penetrating and operating against hardened targets has definitely declined in the post-9/11 era for two main reasons. First, the loss of a secure territorial anchor in Afghanistan, the subsequent arrest of both senior commanders, and the seizure of important components of its financial base have denuded the group of the necessary assets to plan and mount operations on the scale of those undertaken in East Africa in 1998 and New York and Arlington in 2001. Second, al Qaeda can no longer accomplish the type of vertically integrated command and control over international operations—a consequence of the aforementioned loss of haven and leadership—that is so necessary for the successful execution of strategic attacks.

This altered environmental and organizational context has necessarily forced al Qaeda to adopt a broader portfolio of strike options, which now increasingly appear to be focusing on soft targets "farmed out" to the group's global affiliates. As the following breakdown of major al Qaeda-linked incidents post-9/11 indicates (see the RAND-MIPT Terrorism Incident Database), the three years since 2002 have witnessed a significant number of these types of strikes, including assaults against

- hotels (for example, attacks against the Israeli-owned Mombassa Paradise Hotel in November 2002, the U.S.-owned Jakarta Marriott in August 2003, and the Hilton Taba in October 2004)
- bars and discos (for example, the Bali bombings in October 2002, which involved simultaneous explosions inside Paddy's Bar and outside the Sari Nightclub)
- places of worship (for example, strikes against synagogues in Tunisia [Djerba] in March 2002 and Turkey [Istanbul] in November 2003)

- transportation (for example, the Madrid commuter train bombings of March 2004)
- office complexes (for example, the attacks on the headquarters of the Hong Kong and Shanghai Banking Corporation and the building housing the British Consulate,[9] both in Istanbul in November 2003)
- passenger aircraft (for example, the attempted downing of an Israeli charter plane leaving Mombassa in November 2002)
- commercial shipping (for example, the suicide attack against the French-registered *MV Limburg* off the coast of Yemen in November 2002)
- foreign workers and contractors (for example, strikes against a bus transporting French engineers in Karachi in May 2002 and the bombing of an American contractor housing complex in Saudi Arabia in May 2004).[10]

These particular attack choices undoubtedly reflect tactical innovation and pragmatism engendered by the U.S.-led GWOT, which has made it increasingly difficult to conduct more sophisticated, long-range strategic assaults against hardened targets. Although lacking the symbolic prominence of more strategic buildings and bases, these soft venues tend to be characterized by largely unimpeded public access, concentrating large numbers of people in a single space. They are, in other words, easy to attack in a manner that is likely to yield a significant body count.[11] Moreover, given their ease of execution, strikes

---

[9] The preferred target in Istanbul was apparently an American cruise liner; however, the ship had yet to dock when the terrorists were ready to attack, causing them to switch to the British consulate as a fallback.

[10] In addition to these attacks, al Qaeda is believed to have been in the process of preparing a series of bombings against mass transit and other infrastructure in London during 2004. The alleged plots were uncovered as a result of two anti-terrorism operations that linked the alleged plotters to plans to attack economic targets in the United States.

[11] Determining what constitutes a "significant" body count is, of course, entirely subjective. For the purposes of this book, anything over 20 fatalities per attack is deemed to meet this threshold; this figure equates to 20 percent of the number of deaths that have typically been used to connote an act of (conventional) mass destruction terrorism. See Tucker, 2001, p. 8.

against soft targets provide greater scope for locally based cells and supporters (Arab and non-Arab alike) to carry them out, providing al Qaeda with a highly useful "force multiplier" that effectively puts the organization in all places at all times. The increased emphasis on soft targets carries particular relevance for the United States. Since 9/11, concerted efforts have been made to upgrade security provisions around prominent sites, such as the Pentagon, White House, Capitol Building, state legislatures, and foreign diplomatic missions. Special provisions now govern all flights departing from or arriving into Reagan National Airport,[12] while the City of New York has been on a continuous state of heightened orange alert since March 2002 (when the color-coded threat index was first introduced) (Peterson and Meyer, 2004).[13] These initiatives have undoubtedly enhanced the difficulty of attacking prominent landmarks in the continental United States. However in so doing, they have arguably contributed to a process of threat displacement that has heightened the attractiveness of softer targets such as sports stadiums, shopping malls, restaurants, nightclubs, cinema complexes, office buildings, airport departure and arrival areas, and train stations. Moreover for the reasons stated above, the perpetrators of these assaults are as likely to be locally based affiliates as members from "al Qaeda central."

Certainly this has been the trend in other parts of the world, as is evidenced by the attacks on nightclubs in Bali (as opposed to hardened American and Australian embassies[14] in Jakarta), hotels in Taba and Mombassa (as opposed to hitting targets in Israel proper), and

---

[12] Passengers are subjected to rigorous scrutiny on all planes departing to National Airport; moreover, because flight paths pass over prominent sites in the nation's capital, no individual is allowed to leave his or her seat within 40 minutes of taking off or landing.

[13] The U.S. Department of Homeland Security introduced a five-color-coded terrorism warning index in 2002. Known as the Threat Advisory System, the schematic delineates the extant danger of terrorism to the American homeland in the following manner: green—low, blue—guarded, yellow—elevated, orange—high, red—severe. For further details, see U.S. Department of Homeland Security, 2005.

[14] The Australian embassy was bombed in 2004; however, this attack is now known to have been the responsibility of Jemaah Islamyya—a pan-regional Southeast Asian Islamist group—rather than al Qaeda per se.

commuter trains in Madrid (as opposed to diplomatic missions and government buildings in the Spanish capital). In all these cases, attacks have emanated from cells that, while undoubtedly motivated and inspired by al Qaeda, nonetheless have sought to "operationalize" the group's ideological agenda according to their own interpretation and on their own initiative.

In looking to future U.S. attack contingencies, one potentiality that could therefore arise is a growing emphasis on civilian-centric strikes that local affiliates—including American/Western passport holders[15]—can quickly put together and execute on a largely autonomous basis. However, this observation does not preclude the possibility that al Qaeda will seek to attack iconic targets in the continental United States. It is merely that, pragmatically, there may be greater incentive to focus on softer venues. Such a formula for violence will provide al Qaeda with targets and operational modalities that are not only well suited to the constraints of the post-9/11 era, but, more important, ones that can also be readily exploited to *visibly* demonstrate the group's continued durability—both as an ideology and as a concept.

Implications for Public Policy on Terrorism Insurance. The possibility of a sustained and potentially higher al Qaeda attack tempo suggests an obvious implication for public policy on insurance: The requirement for providing financial security to the private sector in the face of ongoing attacks remains. This implies that there continues to be a need for financial protection of the kind that TRIA was intended to encourage. If the act were to sunset, at least in the short run, this would lead to a rise in prices and a decline in take-up rates, while the underlying risk of attacks remains.

---

[15] Two cases in point are (1) Richard Reid (the so-called "shoe bomber"), a UK passport holder who was apprehended in December 2001 after trying to detonate an explosive device on a flight from Paris to Miami; and (2) Jose Padilla, a U.S. citizen detained in May 2002 (and since held as an enemy combatant) for plotting to carry out a radiological attack on the American homeland. For further details on these two individuals and the circumstances surrounding their respective arrests see "Why An Appeals Court Opinion," 2004; "Who Is Richard Reid," 2001; and "Person of the Week," 2002.

This section also describes two other trends about attacks by al Qaeda: (1) the disruption of the network's organizational context has increased the risk to soft targets; and (2) the hardening of high-profile government sites, such as the Pentagon, White House, and foreign diplomatic missions, has inadvertently triggered a process of threat displacement that has further reinforced the risk to less well-protected venues. While there are some soft targets that are public, such as train stations, many are in the private sector, which relies on a functioning insurance system to protect itself from financial losses arising from terrorist attacks. Therefore, to the extent that the sunset of TRIA reduces the supply of terrorism insurance, without additional government intervention after the fact, it also reduces the ability of the economy to be resilient in the aftermath of an attack.

It is important to note that these observations apply only to the trends described in this section and do not imply that TRIA is the best way to structure a system of risk management for losses to the private sector from terrorist attacks. In the final chapter of the report, we summarize and integrate the various trends and their implications for public policy about terrorism insurance.

An Ongoing Emphasis on Economic Attacks

Al Qaeda first realized the potential for this form of terrorism in the wake of the 9/11 attacks. Although the World Trade Center and Pentagon were primarily chosen for their symbolic status as the seat of American commercial and military power, the financial damage wrought by the two strikes was enormous (especially in the former case), negatively affecting New York business[16] and contributing to a massive crisis in the national airline industry that is, arguably, continuing to this day.[17] For bin Laden, 9/11 exposed the United States

---

[16] According to one study conducted by one of New York's leading management consulting firms, the attacks on the twin towers of the World Trade Center cost the city roughly $83 billion in direct economic losses. Figure quoted in Ellis, 2004, p. 123.

[17] U.S. airlines experienced overall revenue losses in excess of $17 billion between September 2001 and the end of 2002, two-thirds of which were tied to reduced passenger manifests post-9/11. See McKenzie, 2003. However, as part of the Air Transportation Safety and Sys-

for what it is—a "paper tiger" that is on the verge of financial ruin and total collapse (much as the USSR was in the late 1980s).[18] Moreover, the attacks graphically underscored the vulnerability of America's highly complex critical infrastructure—the systems deemed essential to the effective day-to-day running of the country[19]—demonstrating how quickly devastating cascading effects can result from single disruptions to networks that have become increasingly interdependent in nature (in this case civil aviation, which was fully grounded for 24 hours and took a full two weeks to regain a semblance of normalcy) (Kunreuther and Michel-Kerjan, 2004b; Michel-Kerjan, 2003, pp. 132–141; and "Civil Aviation Post-9/11/01," 2005).

During the past three years, al Qaeda has sought to give concrete expression to this self-perceived realization by specifically focusing on venues liable to generate disruptive commercial effects, including oil installations, banking institutions, seaports, airports, hotels, prominent tourist hubs, and shipping. A case in point was the 2002 bombing of the French-registered supertanker, *MV Limburg*. The attack was noteworthy not only for its effect on international oil prices[20] and the Yemeni economy[21] but also in its ultimate confirmation of al Qaeda's stated intention to target the financial anchors underpinning the Western capitalist system:

---

tem Stabilization Act (Public Law 107-42), the airlines also have the ability to apply for loans from the federal government and receive federal insurance.

[18] In an interview with *al-Jazeera*, for instance, bin Laden remarked that 9/11 generated billions of dollars in losses to Wall Street, in the daily income of U.S. citizens, in building costs, and to the airline industry. All this damage, he observed was "due to an attack that happened with the success of Allah lasting one hour only." See Flynn, 2004, p. 25.

[19] These are generally taken to include telecommunications, energy, banking, transportation, finance, water systems, emergency services, and agriculture.

[20] In the immediate aftermath of the attack, for instance, the price of Brent crude rose by 48 cents to $28.60 a barrel ("Terrorists Blamed," 2002).

[21] The bombing also had profoundly negative consequences on the Yemeni economy, causing the country to lose an estimated $3.8 million per month in port revenues (Herbert-Burns, 2004, pp. 7–8). See also Richardson, 2004, p. 18; "Maritime Security Measures," 2003, p. 55; "Terrorists Blamed," 2002; and "Who Dunnit?" 2002.

If a boat that didn't cost US$1,000 managed to devastate an oil tanker of that magnitude, so imagine the extent of the danger that threatens the West's commercial lifeline, which is petroleum. The operation of attacking the French tanker is not merely an attack against a tanker, it is an attack against international transport lines (al Qaeda communiqué, October 13, 2002, cited in Richardson, 2004, p. 50).

Al Qaeda's continued focus on commercial jets further underscores the shift to economic targets. While the choice of this particular modus operandi undoubtedly reflects its past use as a successful form of mass casualty terrorism, there is good reason to believe it also implies a perception that such operations will result in additional setbacks to commercial aviation and tourism. Indeed, in December 2003, a number of flights were cancelled from Europe to the United States precisely because of reported attempts by al Qaeda operatives to hijack and destroy planes during the traditionally busy holiday season.[22]

At least rhetorically, there is reason to believe that al Qaeda is interested in continuing its efforts to disrupt the fiscal base of the United States by attacking targets within its borders. Certainly the group's recruitment videos and pamphlets suggest as much in that they specifically urge young Muslims to bleed America dry through repeated (domestic) strikes against key pillars of the country's economy.[23] Moreover, in a video-recorded statement released in October 2004, bin Laden squarely put the thrust of his campaign against the United States in the context of economic war:

> This is in addition to our having experience in using guerrilla warfare and the war of attrition to fight tyrannical superpowers, as we, alongside the mujahidin, bled Russia for 10 years, until it went bankrupt and was forced to withdraw in defeat. . . . So we are continuing this policy in bleeding America to the point of

---

[22] See, for instance, "Possible Plane Plot," 2003; "Threats Ground," 2003; and "Alert Spurs," 2003.

[23] See, for instance, Campbell and Gunaratna, 2003, pp. 73–74; and Eedle, 2002.

bankruptcy (Bin Laden statement reproduced in "Full Transcript," 2004; see also Jehl and Johnston, 2004).[24]

The alleged 2004 plot to target prominent financial institutions in New York, Newark, and Washington, D.C.—including the Stock Exchange, Citicorp Inc., the headquarters of the Prudential Group, the World Bank, and the International Monetary Fund—would also seem to provide at least residual empirical evidence that al Qaeda is actively seeking to attack directly economic targets on U.S. soil. Initial surveillance on each of these venues had apparently been carried out in 2000 and 2001, providing blueprints that government and intelligence sources believe were being used to lay the parameters for a campaign of economic attacks involving truck bombs (interviews, New York Police Department Intelligence and Counter-Terrorism Divisions, 2004–2005; see also Peterson and Meyer, 2004; Meyer, 2004; and Johnston and Lichtblau, 2004).[25]

Implications for Public Policy on Terrorism Insurance. The trends in this section have three implications for public policy on terrorism insurance. The first echoes and reinforces the discussion of the last section, namely that a focus by al Qaeda on attacking the pillars of the economy shifts the risk to the private sector and, therefore, to potential insured targets.

The second implication is that if al Qaeda's goal is to conduct strikes that reverberate through the economy causing cascading, ever-increasing losses, public policymakers need to examine possible financial mechanisms that are available to mitigate these effects. While TRIA was originally justified primarily as a measure to stimulate the economy, insurance also has the effect of promoting resilience in the

---

[24] The importance of these pronouncements lies in al Qaeda's unerring penchant for making good on its threats and turning into reality attacks on the type of targets they highlight for attack.

[25] Information about the 2000 and 2001 surveillance effort first came to light following the seizure of computer discs and documents discovered in Pakistan during July 2004. American authorities feared that these surveys were disseminated to operational al Qaeda cells based in the United States, Pakistan, and the United Kingdom as part of a concerted effort to attack the continental United States before the end of 2004.

aftermath of an attack. Thus, a functioning terrorism insurance system, at least in the context of economic targeting by al Qaeda, should be thought of as not just an economic development mechanism but also as a counterterrorism tool.

As noted in Chapter Two, because terrorism was not identified as a separate risk in commercial property and casualty insurance before 9/11, there was effectively a 100 percent take-up rate for terrorism insurance. This insurance was paid primarily in the category of business interruption ($11 billion), which allowed businesses to continue to function and avoid layoffs while relocating or while lower Manhattan was closed to traffic and in property insurance ($7.5 billion), which allowed businesses to rebuild damaged or destroyed properties (Dixon and Stern, 2004). Without this significant flow of capital into the areas where the attacks occurred, the damage to New York's economy and undoubtedly to the country would have been far greater.

Today, with terrorism insurance take-up rates at approximately one-half of insured commercial assets, it is likely that the role of insurance would be reduced in the recovery from a future attack. As a result, the follow-on effects may be considerably greater to the extent that some firms and companies have not purchased business interruption or property coverage for terrorist attacks. As noted, if TRIA is allowed to sunset, at least in the short term, it is likely that take-up rates will fall as prices rise. Therefore, the insurance system's ability to serve as a cushion against the economic effects of a terrorist attack will be reduced.

In the long run, these considerations suggest that a permanent program of terrorism insurance should have far higher take-up rates than the current system. To this end, the government might consider policies that encourage increased purchase of terrorism insurance, such as tax subsidies and reduced deductibles.[26]

---

[26] Increased deductibles for individual insurance companies do not necessarily mean increased ultimate government payments, since TRIA includes a mechanism for recouping payments through surcharges on insurance in subsequent years. If a company's deductibles are decreased and the industry deductible is increased, this would increase risk sharing across

The third implication is that attacks on critical infrastructure may be particularly effective precisely because they lead to indirect losses for which insurance is not available. Business interruption insurance covers lost income that is caused by a fire or another specific event. It does not cover losses that are the indirect effect of a terrorist attack, such as reduced occupancy in hotels and/or the grounding of airlines.[27] Attacks on networks, such as airports and seaports, lead to indirect effects that are not covered by insurance, and, therefore, businesses cannot readily recover from the resulting losses. Other means of financial risk management may need to be encouraged to mitigate the follow-on economic effects from these types of attacks.

If it facilitates more rapid recovery of the network, it may be that privately owned critical infrastructure facilities should be required to hold terrorism insurance or that its costs should be publicly defrayed. An additional advantage of this policy would be that it would ensure a wide geographic spread of insured facilities, which diversifies the risk and increases the insurability of terrorism. This policy may also facilitate the adoption of security measures if premiums can be lowered for fortified facilities. However, it must be emphasized that this suggestion requires further study since mandatory insurance poses complications that include identifying an insurer of last resort, and the ability to use insurance to incentivize security measures is controversial and may not provide sufficient incentives to pay for costly measures.

Continued Reliance on Suicide Strikes

The ethos of suicide terrorism is firmly embedded in both the ideology and strategy of al Qaeda. Although several other Islamist organi-

---

insurance companies and decrease taxpayer involvement. See forthcoming RAND research by Stephen Carroll, Tom LaTourrette, and Craig Martin on losses and compensation for terrorist attacks.

[27] See *City of Chicago v. Factory Mutual Insurance Company,* U.S. District Court for the Northern District of Illinois, Eastern Division, 2004. The City of Chicago was denied compensation for business interruption resulting from the Federal Aviation Administration's decision to ground air traffic after 9/11, which is discussed in Kunreuther and Michel-Kerjan (2004b).

zations have utilized and justified the use of these tactics (for example, Hamas, Palestinian Islamic Jihad, Hezbollah, and the Al-Aqsa Martyr's Brigade), few have invested so much time and effort in actually *programming* their fighters for death. Reflecting what Juan Cole and others have referred to as a highly effective and pervasive form of collective psychological self-belief (Gunaratna, 2002, p. 7; Cole, 2003), martyrdom has become as much a characteristic trait of al Qaeda as has the belief in, and general endorsement of, global jihad. Indeed to the degree that al Qaeda stresses training of its operatives for missions, the organization appears to actually place greater emphasis on psychological than military preparation, especially in terms of mentally conditioning its cadres to accept (and venerate) their religious obligation to die in the service of Allah.[28] Such self-sacrifice is proclaimed as not only the most expressive way to demonstrate loyalty to the Muslim cause, but also the most direct way to establish a true pioneering vanguard for the Islamic faith (Gunaratna, 2002, pp. 73, 91–92; also see "Al-Qaeda Is Replicating," 2002).

Although al Qaeda's rationalization for martyrdom tends to be couched in religious terms, the overarching emphasis on, and commitment to, this form of aggression is driven by considerations of a far more practical nature. Three factors have been particularly important in this regard:

- Suicide terrorism's potential to elicit a high body count with the minimum of cost.[29]

---

[28] In one seven-minute recruitment video seized by American forces in 2002, al Qaeda gives clear expression to the transcendental dimension of suicide terrorism and the central place it plays in the group. The tape presents various scenes of jihadists in combat, followed by the images of 27 martyrs, 12 of whom are shown in a concluding section celebrating to an accompanying voiceover: "They rejoice in the bounty provided by Allah: And with regard to those left behind who have not yet joined them in their bliss, the martyrs glory in the fact that on them is no fear, nor have they cause to grieve" (Abu Ghaith, 2001).

[29] The Palestinian group Hamas provides a good example. A typical suicide operation undertaken by the organization normally runs to around $150; however, these attacks generally inflict six times the number of deaths and roughly 26 times more casualties than other acts of terrorism. These figures are drawn from the RAND-MIPT Terrorism Incident Database.

- The enormous fear these strikes tend to spark among target audiences, not least by creating an image of an enemy that is at once utterly ruthless and totally undeterrable.
- Martyrdom's proven capacity to radicalize and mobilize additional supporters and recruits.[30]

In the years since 9/11, al Qaeda has been linked to suicide attacks across Europe, Asia, and the Middle East that have collectively killed well in excess of 900 people.[31] The range of targets has been as diverse as the locations, including nightclubs, restaurants, hotels, housing compounds, oil refineries, synagogues, cemeteries, commercial ships, and security establishments. This litany of violence bears stark testimony to a group that clearly continues to view martyrdom as the most effective way of pursuing and prosecuting its war against the West.[32]

America has, of course, already been struck by a major act of suicide terrorism inside its borders—the strikes against the Pentagon and the World Trade Center on September 11. However, since then there have been no repeat attacks, with the country remaining free of what many now consider to be the essential defining trait of the transnational jihadist movement. It is difficult to speculate exactly why this has been the case, although a number of explanations have been advanced, including the following:

- The difficulty of covertly infiltrating suicide operatives into the continental United States, particularly in light of strengthened

---

[30] For more on the practical instrumentalities that underscore suicide terrorism, see Pape, 2003; Sprinzak, 2000; Schweitzer, 2001; and "Martyrdom and Murder," 2004.

[31] This figure is an approximation based on numbers quoted in various government reports, newspaper articles, and analytical assessments.

[32] Indeed, the frequency of suicide strikes has risen markedly since 9/11. While this increase no doubt reflects the emphasis on using affiliates to carry out attacks on soft targets of opportunity (which, as noted in the text, can be executed on both a sustained and largely semi-autonomous basis), it is also indicative of the "positive utility" that this form of terrorism has in terms of cost-benefit ratios.

internal intelligence, border, and custom arrangements instituted over the last three years.

- The problematic nature of (externally) indoctrinating and motivating cadres that may already be in place—a psychological dimension that is absolutely crucial to the systematic perpetration of this type of terrorism.
- The possibility that al Qaeda views martyrdom as contrary to the explicit image of power it seeks to project in the specific U.S. context (that is, the group considers that it has the capability of destroying America's "heart" through more conventional means).[33]

While all these hypotheses warrant consideration—and no doubt contain a measure of truth—one cannot dismiss the possibility of future attacks in the continental United States taking the form of suicide strikes. External barriers can never act as a 100 percent guarantee of security, and there is no way of knowing how jihadist elements that may already be in the country will seek to further the Islamist cause. Moreover, there are certain facets of the domestic U.S. environment that are well "suited" to the perpetration and amplification of martyrdom, which future terrorist threat assessments should at least take into account. Not only does the country represent a target-rich theater in which to act (potential attack venues include everything from cinemas, shopping malls, and sports stadiums to offices, subways, and universities), the psychological effect of suicide bombings could be especially great given the generally risk-averse nature of wider American civil society.

It is also worth bearing in mind that al Qaeda has, again, at least rhetorically, hinted at the possibility of future suicide assaults in the United States. As Sulaiman Abu Ghaith has affirmed: "There are thousands more young followers who look forward to death like Americans look forward to living" (Sulaiman Abu Ghaith, cited in

---

[33] Comments to this effect were made during the *Comparative Government for Homeland Security Senior Executive Course,* Monterey Naval Postgraduate School, June 2004. See also Shrader, 2004.

Islamic-World.Net, 2001). The import of statements such as these lies in the group's unerring penchant for making good on its threats and turning into reality the type of attack profiles it highlights.

Implications for Public Policy on Terrorism Insurance. The observation that al Qaeda is likely to continue to rely on suicide attack modalities is not predictive of the scale or type of attack and, therefore, does not carry the same implications for insurance public policy that the other trends in this chapter carry. While 9/11 was undoubtedly an act of martyrdom of the utmost proportions, more typical suicide truck, car, or human bomb attacks are of considerably smaller magnitude. These types of contingencies, which have been particularly marked in countries such as Israel and Iraq over the last several years, would be completely insurable through private insurance in the United States. They would almost certainly never lead to the scale of property damage, business interruption, or loss of life—even when undertaken as multiple, simultaneous strikes—that would cause TRIA's federal reinsurance provisions and mechanisms to be invoked.

It also seems likely that while insurance companies were reluctant to offer insurance without the federal guarantee after 9/11, there would not be a similar reluctance to cover losses, at an affordable price, due to a campaign of small-scale, conventional martyr attacks. This is because suicide terrorism does not, in general, have the characteristics of concentrated risk and catastrophic loss that 9/11's enormity invoked for the insurance industry. Indeed, the pricing of terrorism insurance for attacks of this type could help to encourage the adoption of security measures, such as private security guards and bag inspections, that advocates of reduced government involvement in terrorism insurance have long emphasized. If such attacks occurred, the federal government may choose to offer assistance to the business owners or the victims to show solidarity, but the structure of such a government intervention would look nothing like TRIA.

The greater risk of a campaign of small-scale suicide attacks against shopping malls, for instance, in the United States lies in the probability of ordinary citizens exhibiting considerably less willingness to patronize establishments at risk. The ramifications of a change in consumer behavior of this sort could have devastating effects on certain sectors of the economy, particularly since these types of consequences—being indirect—would not be covered under most insurance programs.

A Desire to Use CBRN Weapons, but Little Ability to Execute Large-Scale Unconventional Attacks

Al Qaeda has long expressed a direct interest in the offensive employment of CBRN materials. Indeed, in an interview with *Time Magazine* four months after the August 1998 U.S. East African embassy bombings, bin Laden specifically asserted that acquiring weapons of mass destruction (WMD) was a religious duty for all Muslims and one that was fully in accordance with Islamic precepts as defined by Allah. Three years later, testimony given by Jamal Ahmad al-Fadl[34] at a U.S. District Court trial in New York detailed how the al Qaeda leader had attempted to buy an unknown quantity of uranium from a Sudanese source in late 1993 or early 1994, with the deal apparently set at $1.5 million. Although it has never been established if the purchase went ahead, al-Fadl did confirm that he had been shown an engraved cylinder approximately two to three feet tall; that a note written in English, specifying "South Africa" and a serial number, had been passed on to another contact, Abu Hajer; and that he was aware al Qaeda possibly possessed an "electric machine" capable of testing highly enriched uranium (Resch and Osborne, 2001; Weiser, 2001a and b; and "Does al-Qaida Have 20 Suitcase Nukes?" 2002).

Perhaps the clearest indication of bin Laden's zealous interest in CBRN weapons, however, has come in the three years since the 9/11 attacks. Documents, manuals, computer hard drives, and floppy discs recovered from al Qaeda bases in Afghanistan have revealed that the group was not only actively engaged in efforts to acquire WMD but had also been in contact with Pakistani scientists regarding the best

---

[34] Al-Fadl turned himself in to U.S. authorities in 1996, claiming that he was seeking protection after he was caught embezzling funds from various al Qaeda front companies located in Sudan. In exchange, he offered to provide a detailed account of his ties with bin Laden and the various activities that the Saudi had been engaged in while based in Khartoum. See Weiser, 2001b.

means to build such weapons. Supplemental information provided by journalists, security consultants, and former intelligence officials has further shown that al Qaeda at least explored the possibility of obtaining "suitcase nuclear bombs"—portable atomic demolition devices that can be fired from grenade or rocket launchers—from sources in the former Soviet Union and may have been engaged in similar attempts to procure biological and chemical agents stored in the Czech Republic, Iraq, and North Korea. (See, for instance, Ellis, 2004, pp. 122–123; Hayden, 2004; "Journalist Says," 2004; and "Does al-Qaida Have 20 Suitcase Nukes?" 2002.)

No evidence currently exists that al Qaeda has yet been able to translate its undoubted interest in WMD to actual possession. Moreover, the group's current disaggregated and resource-depleted character would seem to preclude the option of its being able to independently manufacture CBRN weapons for large-scale, strategic attacks in the short-to-medium term. These considerations notwithstanding, one cannot and, indeed, should not discount the possibility of more limited strikes being carried out to generate psychological and/or economic (rather than physical) damage. Reports in 2002 that Jose Padilla was in the early stages of planning to detonate a "dirty bomb" (which involves the release of radiological material through a conventional explosion) in an American city and the 2003 discovery of a rudimentary "factory" in London that was experimenting with a ricin recipe[35] both augur that al Qaeda continues to see value in this form of terrorism. While neither the former device nor the latter agent can be considered a true WMD, both have a very real potential to directly affect government policy and public morale: the first by making widespread areas unfit for human habitation and/or employ-

---

[35] For further details on these incidents, see Hutchinson, 2003, p. 34; "Bioterror Plot," 2003; "Bean There," 2003; and McGrory, 2003.

ment,[36] the second by generally heightening the perceived fears associated with the release of highly poisonous substances.[37]

Should a future CBRN attack take place in the United States, it may well follow this general pattern: easy to execute strikes that are cheap, low risk, and designed to elicit social and economic disruption rather than large-scale loss of life per se, but that have a genuine potential to destabilize and disorient. Two types of assault could fit within this context: radiological releases and low-tech biological attacks.

Radiological Releases. One can expect to see an ongoing interest in releasing radiological material through modified dirty bombs. There are myriad sources internal to the United States that could be used for this purpose,[38] ranging from radiation equipment employed in medical facilities to U.S. research stations, commercial sites, and atomic waste storage tanks located at prominent nuclear facilities (Hutchinson, 2003, p. 34; Flynn, 2004, p. 13; Cockburn, 2003; and Wald, 2004).[39] Most of these venues lack the type of rigorous security

---

[36] The main effect of a dirty bomb would be to contaminate large areas with radioactive waste, which, depending on the volume dispersed, could negate the possibility of rehabitation for many years.

[37] Although ricin is highly toxic—less than a milligram would be fatal—it is extremely difficult to disperse in a manner that would affect a large number of people over wide geographic areas. The agent is, thus, suited more for generating psychological effects (or as a means of assassination; ricin was "famously" used to kill Georgi Markov, a Bulgarian émigré in London in 1978, for instance) rather than for mass murder.

[38] It should also be noted that material could be imported from outside. Indeed in late 2003, intelligence reports indicated that Adnan El Shukrijumah, a reputed key al Qaeda operative in North America, had attempted to acquire radioactive components from a 5-megawatt research reactor in Hamilton, Canada, for an attack that was reputedly being planned for the United States in 2004.

[39] Although the Bush administration has made preventing the spread of WMD a top priority, it has slashed funds to dispose of commercially held radioactive materials that could be used in dirty bombs, such as cobalt-160, americium, and cesium-137. Indeed, at the time of this writing, Congress had approved passage of legislation that would allow the Energy Department to leave residual stocks of atomic waste in tanks located in South Carolina and Idaho, instead of pumping it out and preparing it for deep burial. One environmental group has calculated that if as little as one part in 1,000 of this material were allowed to escape (or was deliberately removed) during the next 100 years, local drinking water supplies would be polluted well above allowable standards.

found at military installations (something that is particularly true of radiotherapy clinics), and at least some power plants have already been the locus of accidental atomic releases.[40]

The overall social, political and economic ramifications of a successful radiological attack occurring in the continental United States could be enormous, irrespective of the number of people actually killed. Depending on the sophistication and size of the device, areas as large as tens of square miles could be contaminated at levels above recommended civilian exposure limits. In serious cases, demolition may be the only practical solution for dealing with affected buildings, Should such an event take place in a city such as New York, it would result in huge losses (Richardson, 2004, pp. 51–52). As Stephen Flynn (2004, p. 25) remarks, a radiological release at a major port could be equally if not more costly:

> [A] dirty bomb . . . set off in a seaport would likely kill only a few unfortunate longshoremen. . . . But if there is no credible security system to restore the public's confidence that other containers are safe, mayors and governors throughout the country, as well as the president, will come under withering political pressure to order the shutdown of the intermodal transportation system. Examining cargo in tens of thousands of trucks, trains, and ships to ensure it poses no threat would have devastating economic consequences. When containers stop moving, assembly plants go idle, retail shelves go bare, and workers end up in unemployment lines. A three-week shut down could well spawn a global recession.

The October 2002 lockdown of all 29 ports along the Western U.S. seaboard provides an indication of the type of economic damage that might result from even a temporary closure of major shipping terminals, both nationally and internationally. The work stoppage, which resulted from a labor dispute between unions and management and lasted nearly two weeks, delayed more than 200 ships carrying 300,000 containers. The direct cost to the American economy associ-

---

[40] The Fernald plant in Ohio, for instance, has a history that includes cumulative releases of at least 500 tons of toxic uranium dust.

ated with cargo disruptions alone has been estimated at $467 million, while the month-long process of clearing subsequent freight backlogs is estimated to have removed between 0.4 and 1.1 percent of nominal gross domestic product from prominent Asian exporters such as Hong Kong, Singapore, and Malaysia (Richardson, 2004, p. 66; see also Organization for Economic Cooperation and Development, 2003, pp. 17–18; and Department of Foreign Affairs and Trade, 2003).

The United States has already confronted the potential specter of a dirty bomb. In June 2002, the federal government announced that it had arrested an American citizen suspected of having established links with al Qaeda and in the process of developing plans to explode a uranium-enriched radiological device. While U.S. officials have admitted the plot had probably not developed much past the discussion stage, they do believe that substantial initial surveillance had taken place on various alternative attack locations, including in the region of the Capitol building (Richardson, 2004, pp. 56–58; Blanche, 2005; Lewis, 2005; "The Dirty Bomb Suspect," 2002; Lane, 2004; "Officials," 2002; and Ryan, 2005).

Low-Technology Biological Attacks. Low-tech biological assaults are also conceivable. While several scenarios are possible, attacks against the agricultural sector could well pose the most serious threat, given their ease of management and potential socioeconomic fallout (both of which fit well with the general evolutionary dynamic of al Qaeda in the post-9/11 era). Small- and medium-scale food processing and packing plants are especially vulnerable. Thousands of these facilities exist across the country, the bulk of which exhibit uneven internal quality control,[41] questionable bio-surveillance, and highly transient, unscreened workforces. Entry and exit controls are not always adequate (and occasionally do not exist at all), and even basic

---

[41] In 2002, the Bush administration introduced plans to upgrade the screening of workers employed at food processing plants and packing facilities. It is not clear, however, how comprehensive these screening checks will be and to what extent they will apply to the thousands of small- and medium-scale plants that exist throughout the United States (which, because of a lack of federal inspectors, necessarily operate on a system of self-regulation).

measures such as padlocking storage rooms may not be practiced. This lack of concerted and uniform security has served to increase the possibility of orchestrating a toxic/bacterial food-borne attack, which even in a limited form could trigger widespread psychological angst and social panic. Indeed, because most processed food is distributed to catchment areas within a matter of hours, a single case of chemical or biological adulteration could have significant latent ongoing effects, particularly if the source of the problem was not immediately apparent[42] and acute or chronic ailments resulted (Chalk, 2004, pp. 11, 16, and 26).

An act of agro-bioterrorism might additionally take the form of a viral strike directed against the lucrative U.S. cattle industry[43]—which would also fit well with al Qaeda's general emphasis on delivering a crippling blow to the American economy. Weaponizing a disease such as foot and mouth—the agricultural equivalent of smallpox given its rate of subject-to-subject transmission—is neither difficult nor expensive, and because the microbe is non-zoonotic in nature, it would not require any substantive containment procedures or personal protective equipment. The means for disseminating foot-and-mouth disease could be as simple as scraping a viral sample directly onto a cow or merely introducing the agent into a silage bin at an animal fair or auction barn. Because the disease is so contagious and given the extremely concentrated and intensive nature of contemporary American livestock farming practices, a multi-focal outbreak across several states may well ensue. The U.S. Department of Agriculture has concluded that a catastrophe of this sort would cost the country billions of dollars in lost beef exports and/or trade sanctions and could possibly preclude a full return to the international market for several years, if not indefinitely (see Chalk, 2004).

---

[42] Quickly identifying and containing the source of a specific food contaminant introduced (deliberately or by accident) at small- and medium-scale processing plants are problematic, since many of these facilities neither keep accurate records of their distribution network nor have concerted product-recall plans in place.

[43] Dairy and cattle farmers earn, on average, between $50 billion and $54 billion a year through beef and dairy sales.

To be sure, neither a radiological nor a low-tech biological attack would generate the type of heightened and prolonged fear and/or damage that an attack deliberately geared to kill and maim would entail. That said, each retains a genuine potential to disorient and destabilize and, as such, could be viewed as attractive to terrorists in terms of exacerbating the social upheaval caused by more traditional civilian-centric bombings. The mere ability to employ cheap and relatively unsophisticated means to undermine a state's economic base—and possibly overwhelm its public-management resources—endows both tactics with a positive cost-benefit payoff that might well be of interest to al Qaeda, particularly as it struggles to compensate for reduced operational opportunities in the post-9/11 era.

Implications for Public Policy on Terrorism Insurance. The possibility of a radiological attack in the United States exposes perhaps the greatest weakness of the terrorism insurance market. As noted in the introduction, TRIA allows insurers to exclude CBRN, and, in general, only workers' compensation insurance, under state law in every state, is still required to offer coverage.[44] As a result, exclusions for radiological attacks on property and business interruption policies are common (Congressional Budget Office, 2005, p. 2).

The overall economic ramifications of a successful dirty bomb attack occurring on American soil would be enormous irrespective of the number of people actually killed. Depending on the size and sophistication of the device employed, an area as large ten square miles could conceivably be contaminated above recommended civilian exposure limits. In serious cases, demolition may be the only practical solution for dealing with affected buildings; should an event of this sort take place in a city such as New York, it would result in huge losses (Richardson, 2004, pp. 51–52).

There is good reason for insurers, who generally seek to avoid open-ended liability, to wish to exclude radiological attacks. For in-

---

[44] This aspect of workers' compensation has raised considerable concern about the sunset of TRIA from workers' compensation insurers, who cannot limit coverage and fear that in the case of a CBRN attack without a backstop, they have elevated risk of insolvency. See Dixon et al., 2004.

stance, while the elevated risk of cancer or other health conditions for individuals exposed to this type of assault may not be great, it would be difficult to demonstrate that health conditions experienced by exposed individuals were not, in fact, caused by the dirty bomb. Just as problematic would be determining how many people were actually exposed to the elevated levels of radiation from the dirty bomb. Finally, decontamination of several blocks of an urban area is likely to be both extraordinarily expensive and largely experimental, not the least because cleaning contingencies of this kind have never been needed or practiced in the United States. Given these considerations, the difficulty of predicting the ultimate losses involved in this type of attack makes coverage difficult to price.

The upshot is that a radiological attack in an urban core would likely lead to catastrophic levels of uninsured business interruption and property losses. The financial risk possibly resulting from an attack of this sort should, as a result, be deemed significant (U.S. GAO, 2004, p. 11).

Contamination of the food supply is not likely to have major implications for insurance. Similar to the network attacks described earlier, this type of assault would lead to economic losses that are typically not covered by insurance. As with other attacks involving cascading, indirect effects, these uninsured losses could pose considerable financial risk.

CHAPTER FOUR

Homegrown Terrorist Threats to the United States

TRIA does not cover terrorist attacks perpetrated by domestic terrorist groups. Therefore, trends in homegrown extremism are highly relevant to assessments of whether the architecture of the contemporary terrorism insurance system is appropriately aligned with underlying threat contingencies as they are occurring in the United States.

Unlike close allied countries such as the United Kingdom and Spain,[1] the United States does not presently suffer from a concerted homegrown terrorist threat. That said, developing imperatives stemming from anti-globalization (AG) do appear to be providing a radical domestic context for galvanizing the militancy of both the far right as well as those driven by more specific extremist environmental agendas.

What Is the Context for the Evolving Threat?

The AG movement first emerged as an inchoate collection of interests ranging from international debt relief and civil rights to championing the cause of Mumia Abu-Jamal, the former Black Panther on death row in Pennsylvania for the death of a police officer. Over the last few years, however, the movement has begun to take on a more coherent worldview. At its core is opposition to corporate power and the as-

---

[1] In Spain, the main threat emanates from ETA; in the UK, it emanates from the residual splinters of the Provisional Irish Republican Army—notably the Real IRA—as well as from right-wing xenophobic organizations such as Combat 18.

sumed socioeconomic and political dislocations that are perceived to follow in its wake. In addition, anti-globalists directly challenge the intrinsic qualities of capitalism, charging that in the insatiable quest for growth and profit, the philosophy is serving to destroy the world's ecology, indigenous cultures, and individual welfare ("Anti-Globalization," 2000). It is in this context that several commentators have described AG as a de-facto "new, new left," drawing comparisons to the "summer of barricades" that swept across Paris, France, in 1968 (see, for instance, von Sternberg, 2000).

A common thread running through both these "ideological" tenets is that globalization and capitalism inevitably lead to illegitimate and unjust concentrations of public, state, and private power. AG advocates forcefully reject the argument that trans-border trade, investment, technology, and information flows help to enhance the human condition, charging, by contrast, that they exacerbate inequality[2] and foster resentment and conflict. Self-interest and ideology are seen to be the main drivers behind globalization, fueling the germination of a liberal pro-market consensus that neither acknowledges nor cares for the needs of the weak and dispossessed (Stanley Hoffmann, 2002, pp. 107–110; and Stiglitz, 2002).

In short, while the specialization and integration of economic power inherent in globalization may make it possible to increase aggregate wealth, the logic of pure capitalism will always work against the notion of universal social justice. As one prominent AG polemicist put it:

> [P]olitical freedom without economic freedom is meaningless. This shared understanding is one of the rallying points for this new international gathering of dissidents, conjured into existence by a capitalism more powerful and unchecked than anything we have seen for a century. . . . Freedom—sovereignty—is about the

---

[2] In support of this assertion, anti-globalists cite figures produced by the World Health Organization and United Nations Development Program showing that the net worth of the world's richest 200 individuals exceeds that of the world's poorest 2.5 billion people. See Pitts, 2002, p. 180.

right to decide your economic, as well as your political, destiny (Kingsworth, 2003).

Given This Context, What Does It Suggest for the Nature of Future Attacks?

Although anti-globalists have been associated with marches, demonstrations, and other acts of civil disobedience in the United States,[3] rank and file activists, for the most part, have eschewed engaging in concerted violent actions, let alone full-blown terrorism. The real threat of the movement lies more in the effects that it appears to be having on anarchist, and, especially, far-right, and radical environmental imperatives. We discuss this effects below.

Anarchism

Anarchism, which has its roots in the 19th century philosophies of Russian theorists such as Michael Bakunin, essentially aims at achieving self-liberation from arbitrarily applied institutions of governance and order (The Anarchist FAQ Editorial Collective, 2005; see also Chalk, 1996, p. 2). Although the ideology is not intrinsically violent, radicals associated with the contemporary manifestation of the movement—which received a major fillip in the mid-1990s following the publication of "Unabomber" Ted Kaczynski's distinctly anti-industrial political manifesto[4]—have increasingly been prepared

---

[3] Notable examples include riots and marches organized to coincide with the 2003 World Bank and International Monetary Fund meetings in Washington, D.C., as well as the 2004 National Conventions of the Republican and Democratic parties in New York and Boston, respectively; the 2000 International Society for Animal Genetics conference in Minneapolis; and the 2000 TransAtlantic Business Dialogue in Cincinnati. For further details of these events see FBI, 2001, pp. 2–3. The FBI refers to these venues and meetings as politically charged special events.

[4] In 1995, the *New York Times* and *Washington Post* jointly agreed to publish the 35,000 word political manifesto of Ted Kaczynski, whose unilateral campaign of letter bombings were linked to three deaths and nearly two dozen injuries over a 17-year period. Kaczynski's statement revealed a complex ideology that revolved around an idiosyncratic mixture of Luddite (a reference to the textile workers who rose up in rebellion in England during the 19th century to protest the introduction of weaving machines in the country) and anarchist

to attack symbols of state order, including politicians, judges, and the police (The Anarchist FAQ Editorial Collective, 2005). Anarchists have also emerged as key instigators of large-scale civil disobedience, playing a prominent role in organizing disruptions of the 2003 World Bank and International Monetary Fund meetings in Washington, D.C., as well as the 2004 National Conventions of the Republican and Democratic parties in New York and Boston.[5]

To be sure, the heightened activism of these militants has been availed by the general distraction of local law enforcement and intelligence to arguably more serious imported terrorist threats connected with al Qaeda and the loosely affiliated international jihadist movement. However, there is little question that anarchists have been animated by the growing influence of AG, particularly the assertion that international trade and commerce are, in fact, a mask designed to hide and covertly advance U.S. global economic, cultural, and political power (Stanley Hoffmann, 2002, p. 108). Aspects of American foreign policy, such as the GWOT and the invasion and subsequent occupation of Iraq, are singled out as emblematic of this "reality" and confirmation that Washington is pursuing a single-minded policy aimed at establishing its hegemony in key strategic regions of the world.

The major danger of AG-inspired anarchism lies in the potential militancy of fringe elements—or socially unbalanced "lone wolves"— who, having drifted toward violent confrontation with the state, begin to adopt more explicit terrorist designs. In Europe, this type of radicalization has already occurred, with the establishment of groups such as the Italian Proletarian Nuclei for Communism and its sister movement, the Bologna-based Informal Anarchist Federation. The former was implicated in a reputed bomb plot against British Prime

---

ideals essentially aimed at curtailing and ultimately rolling back industrial technocracy. For an interesting account of the activities and background of the Unabomber, see Ottley, 2005. See also Taylor, 1998, appendixes A and B; and "Post, Times," 1995. Excerpts of Kaczynski's manifesto can be accessed online at http://www.usatoday.com/news/index/una6.htm (as of June 2005).

[5] Comments made during the *Comparative Government for Homeland Security Course,* Monterey Naval Postgraduate School, September 27–29, 2004.

Minister Tony Blair while he was visiting Sardinia in August 2004, while the latter took responsibility for a series of rudimentary parcel explosive devices that were posted to senior European Union officials earlier in 2004 (Willan, 2004; "Italian Anarchists," 2004; "Letter Bombs," 2004).

Although the United States has yet to experience this level of directed anarchist action, a loosely networked cadre of militants has emerged in the guise of the "Black Bloc." Often masked and armed with clubs, these radicals are largely responsible for instigating the street protests of the sort witnessed in Washington, D.C., during 2003 and New York and Boston in 2004. FBI domestic risk assessments now routinely single out the Black Bloc and other Kaczynski-type anarchists, warning that they are assuming heightened influence over the American protest population and possibly directing it toward more civilian-centric violence.[6]

The Far Right

The threat of U.S.-based, right-wing extremists first became apparent in 1995 with the bombing of the Alfred P. Murrah Federal building in Oklahoma City. Perpetrated by Timothy McVeigh—a 28-year-old U.S. Army veteran (who has since been executed)—to commemorate the second anniversary of the FBI's bloody assault on the Branch Davidian's compound in Waco, Texas,[7] the attack remains the worst act of homegrown domestic terrorism to have ever taken place in the United States (Weiner, 1995; Applebome, 1995; and Wilson, 1995).[8] During the course of the intervening nine years, numerous right-wing/xenophobic militias have emerged, variously championing a combination of revolutionary, racist, and anti-Semitic doctrines.

---

[6] Comments made during the Free Trade Area of the Americas Annual Meeting, Miami, Florida, November 16–21, 2003. See also Davidson-Smith, 1998, p. 3.

[7] McVeigh apparently interpreted the 1993 assault in Waco, which resulted in the deaths of 74 people—as well as the siege of an alleged white supremacist's rural cabin at Ruby Ridge, Idaho, a year earlier—as part of a wider federal government plan aimed at outlawing and seizing all privately owned firearms. See Bruce Hoffman, 1999, p. 105. For a detailed account of the incidents, see also Tabor and Gallagher, 1995.

[8] The bombing killed 169 and injured 500 others.

According to a 2004 report by the Anti-Defamation League, these organizations currently have cells in at least 32 states across America, with a total estimated membership in the range of 5,000 (Anti-Defamation League, 2004; see also Greenberg, 2004).

At heart, these groups are opposed to any form of government above the county level, with an unbending commitment to uphold the right of the individual to bear arms and a general obsession with ensuring religious and racial purification of the United States, including the purging of all Zionist influences from the country (Bruce Hoffman, 1999, p. 111). Globalization has sharpened and galvanized these imperatives—both on account of the concentration of state power that it entails and because of a conviction that the move to foster international finance, trade, and commerce is, in fact, an American-led conspiracy, conducted by, and for the benefit of, Jewish capitalists. Indeed the National Alliance, one of North America's largest neo-Nazi groups, has now created an "Anti-Globalism Action Network" that specifically affirms white nationalists as both anti-capitalist and anti-establishment for racial, economic, and sovereignty reasons (see, for instance, Nowotny, 2002; and Anti-Defamation League, 2002).

To be sure, much of the railing against globalization is undoubtedly opportunistic in nature, aimed at attracting a broader cross-section of recruits. However, the explicit adoption of AG rhetoric may also be indicative of deeper trends within the extreme right, reflecting a possible ideological convergence with parts of the far left.[9] Certainly this appears to have been the case in Western Europe, particularly in France and Germany, each of which has been identified as the new locus for a "brown-green-red" alliance that attacks Jews and

---

[9] Ideological affinity between the extreme right and far left is not without precedent. During the 1900s, for instance, political extremists ostensibly at odds with one another, in fact, often shared and enunciated a common outlook. In the interwar period in Germany, for instance, certain members of the extreme right described the Soviet Union in approving terms as an "anti-capitalist, anti-liberal beacon" for the world. Similarly, during the 1960s, the American Nazi Party found common cause with the left-leaning Nation of Islam, whose leader, Elijah Muhammad, praised white opponents of "race mixing." See Furet, 1999, p. 203; and Clegg, 1997, pp. 152–153.

Israel in racist, anti-capitalist, and anti-colonialist terms (Strauss, 2003; Communauté Online, 2003).

If, in fact, the U.S. radical right has begun to explicitly (as opposed to rhetorically) embrace an agenda of this sort, one can expect to see increasing militant attention given to venues that have not traditionally been part of this extremist mindset. Multinational companies and institutions perceived as spearheading cross-border trade and capital transactions are likely to be especially singled out on account of their alleged role in propagating and further entrenching the "American Zionist Occupation Government" (ZOG), which has long been a target of groups such as the U.S. Aryan Movement (see below).

The residual threat posed by the far right needs to be observed closely. These organizations have a clear penchant for violence, something that was visibly reflected in the Oklahoma bombing and that has been further evidenced in several subsequent terrorist plots, including strikes involving biological agents.[10] Moreover, the amorphous, networked character of the overall militia movement (which is based on the principle of leaderless resistance),[11] as well as the religious/theological undertones that characterize its existence, arguably invalidates the political, moral, and organizational constraints that commonly mitigate extremist predilections toward mass killings and murder. Such groups take on many of the characteristics of fundamentalist religious organizations and, as such, tend to adopt similar mechanisms of violence legitimization (see, for instance, Chalk, 2000, pp. 15–16).

---

[10] For more on these plots see Bruce Hoffman, 1999, pp. 109–100; and Carus, 1999, chapter 7.

[11] The concept of leaderless resistance, the most comprehensive version of which is advanced in the writings of Louis Beam, offers an alternative to orthodox, pyramid-type organizational structures. The main aim is to base a group on so-called phantom cell networks that operate completely independently of one another but that are able, through the combined force of their action, to precipitate a chain reaction that eventually leads to a national revolution. Beam actually credits a retired U.S. military officer, Colonel Ulius Amoss, with first developing the idea of leaderless resistance in 1962. Amoss, according to Beam, saw this diffuse structure as the most effective way to resist the threat of a communist takeover in the United States. For further details, see Beam, 1992.

The Aryan Movement provides a good example. This loosely structured right-wing milieu brings together an amalgam of white supremacists who have openly justified the use of extreme violence to exterminate the U.S. Jewish population as part of the overall drive to create a pure, unadulterated "Aryan republic." Most of these radicals find individual justification for their deeds and beliefs in the philosophy of William Pierce, a self-proclaimed "race separatist" and author of *The Turner Diaries*. Believed to have influenced the thinking of McVeigh, Pierce's 1978 futuristic novel openly advocates a highly militant, open-ended agenda to purge what is seen as a corrupt and spiritually bankrupt American society:

> We do not need to reason with the monster; we need to put a bullet into its brain and hammer a stake through its heart. If that means blood and chaos and battling with the enemy from house to house in burning cities throughout our land—then, by God, it is better that we get on with it now than later.

The latent danger of right-wing, globalist-inspired terrorism taking place in the United States was given concrete expression in 2002, following the discovery of an extensive weapons storage facility in Noonday, East Texas. Included in the arms dump were 500,000 rounds of ammunition, 65 pipe bombs, briefcases that federal investigators believed were going to be wired for remote detonation, and 800 grams of almost pure cyanide. Forensic analyses later showed that had this latter compound been mixed with acid, it would have created an explosive charge large enough to kill everyone within a 30,000-square-foot facility (Gold, 2004). One of those arrested and charged in connection with the cache was Edward Feltus, who, according to an FBI affidavit, testified to being a member of the New Jersey Militia. Together with the affiliated New Jersey Committee of Safety, this shadowy group explicitly condemns the growing power of the federal government, claiming that Washington (as presently configured) and the United Nations are jointly seeking to impose a compulsory multiculturalism that is directed against those "bold enough to assert their particular identities against globalization and homogenization" (The New Jersey Committee of Safety, undated).[12]

Radical Environmentalism

According to U.S. law enforcement, radical environmentalism currently poses the most visible homegrown threat to the national security of the United States. As recently as June 2004, the FBI designated "eco-terrorism"—the use of or threat to use violence in protest of harm inflicted on animals[13] and the world's biosphere—as the country's number one militant challenge emanating from inside its own borders. Radical environmentalism covers an eclectic range of individuals and causes, although most find expression and representation in the Earth Liberation Front (ELF). Since first emerging as an extremist entity in 1994,[14] this highly decentralized group[15] is esti-

---

[12] See also the official web site of the New Jersey Militia at http://www.njmilitia.org. The New Jersey Committee of Safety was cofounded by the New Jersey Militia and the Association Seeking to Preserve Individual Rights for Everyone.

[13] Although radical environmentalism originated as a movement dedicated to preserving "Mother Earth" from rapacious degradation and exploitation, it quickly evolved to take on a wider, more inclusive agenda. The cause of animal rights, in particular, came to be viewed as part and parcel of general ecological (anti-humanist) imperatives. Since the late 1990s, most commentators agree there has been little practical distinction between the objectives of environmental protection and the aims of groups such as the Animal Rights Militia, the Animal Liberation Front, Stop Huntingdon Animal Cruelty, and the People for the Ethical Treatment of Animals. See, for instance, Taylor, 1998, pp. 6–10.

[14] The ELF originally emerged as a radical offshoot of the earlier Earth First! movement, which was founded in 1980 as a millenarian movement advocating both nonviolent and more direct acts of civil disobedience to preserve U.S. wilderness. For a good overview of the ELF's "parent" organization, see Lee, 1995.

[15] One of the defining traits of the ELF lies in its unintegrated and nonhierarchical character, a structure that closely resembles the workings of leaderless resistance as advanced by Louis Beam (see earlier footnote and Beam, 1992). The group has no clearly defined leader and is devoid of an official member roster. If an individual wishes to participate in the "struggle," all that is required is a physical demonstration of action made in accordance with ELF directives—all of which appear on the ELF official web page. This disaggregated structure is seen as offering two important advantages to the ELF. Philosophically it squares well with the worldview of the group, which claims only the "work" of highly decentralized societies as its own. Practically, it has greatly compounded the difficulty of carrying out effective police and intelligence surveillance of those actively engaged in planning or carrying out acts of ecoterror and sabotage. This both has limited the ability of law enforcement authorities to gain an accurate picture of the intentions or capabilities of the ELF and has complicated legal

mated to have caused between $35 million and $45 million in direct property damage, operating in a geographic arc that has embraced Washington State, Oregon, California, Arizona, New York, Minnesota, Pennsylvania, and Indianapolis (see, for instance, Makarenko, 2003, pp. 28–30; Patricia Brown, 2003; Philipkoski, 2004; and Bell, 2004).

Contemporary radical environmentalism essentially draws on and amalgamates two main concepts (Lee, 1995, pp. 113–116; and Eagan, 1996, pp. 2–4):

- "Biocentrism"—which regards all living organisms on earth as equal and deserving of moral rights and respect.
- "Deep ecology"—which calls for a general rollback of civilization and industrialization, the removal of pathogenic species (including, presumably, rapacious humans), and the restoration of the ecological balance.

For a group such as the ELF, saving the roughly 10 percent of American wilderness that remains is not enough. The goal is, and can only ever be, to restore the environment to its entirety: to recreate ecosystems that have been despoiled by the immoral and exploitative actions of the human race. This objective is to be achieved by adopting an uncompromising stance on the environment and by emphasizing direct action. Lobbying and legal forms of protest are viewed as biased in favor of government and industry (Manes, 1990; Nauess, 1998, pp. 128–131; Carpenter, 1990; Toffler, 1990; and Home, 1990).

Militancy has long been justified as instrumental to this ideological and operational pursuit. According to the ELF's ostensible spokesman, Craig Rosebraugh, no social movement in the United States has ever attained its goals through nonviolence. More to the point, he asserts such an option is simply not a luxury that the ELF (or the human race) can afford: "Today the threat to life on the

---

efforts aimed at establishing responsibility for criminal acts perpetrated in the name of environmental protection. See ELF, 2001, pp. 2–3.

planet is so severe that political violence must be implemented in justice pursuits" (Rosebraugh, 2001; see also Rosebraugh, 2003).

Radical environmentalists have used a variety of tactics in the name of ecological protection, all of which the FBI designate as examples of "special interest terrorism" (see, for instance, Freeh, 2001; and Philipkoski, 2004). The most common form of aggression has been arson, which has typically been carried out using crude incendiary devices, such as birthday candles and/or sponge wicks attached to plastic jugs filled with gasoline. On occasion, however, militants have employed more sophisticated delayed timer bombs, the reputed schematics for which are set out in a 20-page ecoterror "how-to" manual that also includes instructions on how to build mortars and grenades (Davidson-Smith, 1998, p. 5; Taylor, 1998, pp. 8–10).

Tree spiking has been another favored tactic—a process that involves driving long metal shards into trees scheduled for harvesting on public lands. Although the spikes do not cause harm themselves, on contact with a chain saw or mill blade, they could cause serious injury and are thus used to deter loggers from entering forests and wooded areas. Trees are chosen at random and there is effectively no way of differentiating one that is spiked from one that is not (Eagan, 1996, p. 6).[16]

Destruction of general logging infrastructure (collectively known as "monkey-wrenching") has also been emphasized to either delay felling operations and/or impose heavy economic costs on logging companies. Various acts of more basic vandalism have accompanied this high-profile sabotage—targeting both commercial and private properties and typically involving smashing windows, glue-sealing door locks, and spray painting graffiti on buildings with the message "Stop Urban Sprawl" (See Lee, 1995, pp. 116–119; Davidson-Smith, 1998, p. 5; and Makarenko, 2003, pp. 29–30).

Finally, in crossover actions with animal rights extremists (see earlier footnote on animal rights), militants have engaged in product

---

[16] Indicative of the potential harm that tree spiking can cause was the severe maiming of a 23-year-old mill worker in 1987 who lost his teeth, cheek, and part of his jaw after jagged metal shards from a splintered saw tore through his face.

contamination, employee intimidation, and the mailing of contaminated razor blades allegedly laced with rat poison or AIDS-infected blood. A recent variation of this latter technique has been the use of return addresses for individuals and firms accused of engaging in similar abuses against the environment, thus ensuring that if the original recipient does not accept the letter, it will still be sent to an "appropriate" target (Davidson-Smith, 1998, pp. 3–8).

AG is a principal factor in common with the extreme right that appears to be driving the operational designs of radical environmentalism. Advocates of the movement now routinely articulate an anti-materialist worldview, decrying corporate greed as possibly the greatest threat to the planet and its life. Indeed, in the view of certain contemporary ELF theorists, much of the environmental struggle to date has been misconceived specifically because it has overlooked the priority of targeting capitalism and the unrestrained, selfish discretionary spending that it is necessarily seen to entail (ELF, 2001, p. 4).

The growing nexus between radical environmentalism and AG is reflected in a menu of targets that now covers an extremely broad spectrum of corporate, public, and private sector interests. Apart from facilities and businesses that are judged to be detrimental to nonrenewable resources, animal welfare, and the general planetary biosphere (for example, logging companies, forestry stations, wilderness recreational firms, urban developers, and scientific research laboratories), a wide range of venues that are regarded as emblematic of the international capitalist "syndrome" have additionally been singled out for aggression, including the following:

- Luxury homes and mansions along the U.S. Eastern Seaboard, which are personified as epitomizing the selfishness that ranges across America's modern well-to-do population.[17]
- Multinational companies, such as Shell Oil, McDonalds, Starbucks, Gap, and Nike, which are variously accused of exploita-

---

[17] Notable in this regard were a series of arson attacks against luxury homes in Mount Sinai, New York, during 2000, which collectively caused $2 million in damage. See Makarenko, 2003, p. 29.

tive labor practices, union busting, and human rights violations in the developing world.

- Organizations deemed to be at the heart of global trade and commerce and irreconcilably beholden to the so-called "Washington–New York" capitalist consensus.[18]

The short- to medium-term evolution of the radical environmental movement will almost certainly continue to be informed by the growing affinity with AG. Specifically, one can expect to see three interrelated developments taking place over the next five years.

Ideologically, the goal of ecological preservation is likely to fully morph with the wider imperative of AG. This transformation, combined with growing discontent over a variety of U.S. foreign policy decisions—ranging from the war in Iraq to Washington's rejection of the Rio Summit agreement on curbing greenhouse gas emissions—could lead to the emergence of a new radical left-wing fringe across American society that is jointly directed against "big business," "big money," corporate power, and uncaring government.

Organizationally, the trend toward a more inclusive ideological agenda is liable to be reflected in moves to formally institutionalize ties with the radical right[19] and, possibly, other like-minded single-issue causes such as pro-life.[20] These links will additionally augment

---

[18] See, for instance, "Anti-Globalization," 2000, pp. 2–3; and Makarenko, 2003, pp. 28–30. It is important to note, however, that targets are not simply selected according to their symbolic or political value. Environmental activists also emphasize venues that are gauged to be most vulnerable to attack and sabotage. In this way, organizations such as the ELF act very much like bodies of flowing water, frequently opting for the course of least resistance.

[19] Residual contacts between environmentalism and the far right do have a history. During the 19th century, for instance, nature worship, nationalism, and ecology were all central pillars of a broader European cultural revolt directed against modernity, liberalism, and capitalism. Deep ecology has also been mixed with brands of authoritarianism, perhaps most notoriously in Germany where calls have been made for a "Green Adolph." For further details on these links, see Biehl and Staudenmaier, 1995.

[20] The principal pro-life group in the United States is the Army of God, which has been linked to several acts of violence against abortion clinics, including the assassinations of doctors. See Davidson-Smith, 1998, pp. 5–6.

the popular base of radical environmentalism and further "muddy" assumptions about its accepted action parameters.

Finally, operationally, militant ecologists will almost certainly assume an increasingly prominent role in civil disobedience directed against perceived symbols of global capitalism and corporate greed, potentially leading the call for targeted aggression in the name of anti-humanist and anarchist ideals. Washington, D.C., New York, Chicago, and Seattle will be the most affected areas because they either represent the locus of American politico-economic power or play host to prominent conglomerate interests such as Boeing, Microsoft, and Sears.

Implications for Public Policy on Insurance

While al Qaeda has been the overwhelmingly dominant focus of U.S. anti-terrorism activities since 9/11, the Oklahoma City bombing clearly illustrates that large-scale attacks can result from homegrown American extremists. In comparison to 9/11, this latter event was perpetrated against a federal government target; therefore, the implications for private-sector insurance were not significant. However, in the ten years since Oklahoma City, the prevailing trends within the domestic terrorist environment have been toward AG, which carries a clear threat to private-sector corporate interests, especially large multinational businesses. The animosity of radical environmentalists and anarchists to corporate capitalism and cross-border trade is perhaps the most obvious manifestation of this tendency, with groups such as the ELF already engaging in highly costly attacks against a range of commercial venues.[21] The nexus with AG is arguably less de-

---

[21] One of the most economically costly domestic terrorist acts to have ever been carried out in the United States was the 1998 firebombing of the Vail ski resort in Colorado; jointly claimed by the ELF and the Animal Liberation Front, the attack resulted in $12 million worth of damage. See Riley, 1998; "Environmental Arson," 1999; and Sullivan, 1998. Other notable arson incidents attributed to environmental/animal rights militants include a 1996 firebombing of a U.S. Forest Service ranger district in Oakridge, Oreg., resulting in losses that have since been calculated in excess of $9 million; a 1997 torching of an animal slaugh-

veloped among those in the far right, though it is clearly there; what is more, organizations motivated by extreme racist, anti-Semitic, and xenophobic beliefs have shown a clear penchant for the type of catastrophic violence that would carry direct ramifications for terrorism insurance.

Whether the threat emerges from the Christian Patriot Militia, the Black Bloc, the ELF, or some other AG-inspired movement, all exist in much the same operational environment as al Qaeda. As documented in Chapter Three, for example, the increased hardening of public-sector targets in response to potential jihadist strikes is likely to shift risk to private-sector targets. This has relevance for both imported and homegrown threat contingencies and will, by default, reinforce the overall exposure of commercial venues that directly depend on insurance.

Assaults perpetrated by a purely domestic entity would not be covered by the TRIA framework, which defines certified actions as those "carried out by an individual or individuals acting on behalf of any foreign source person or foreign interest" (U.S. Congress, 2002). Despite this, many insurers are making domestic terrorism coverage available, and a majority of those who are insured with TRIA-related coverage have also been purchasing domestic attack coverage (see Marsh Inc., 2004, p. 7; Congressional Budget Office, 2005, p. 7). Overall, while there will be some coverage in a domestic attack, take-up rates for domestic terrorism insurance will be lower than for TRIA-covered terrorist attacks, and a catastrophic attack of this sort also carries with it an elevated risk of insolvency for the insurers involved. Thus, a significant gap exists in the current system for man-

---

terhouse in Redmond, Calif., which destroyed $1.3 million in property and equipment; a 2002 attack on a forest ranger station in Irvine, Pa., which caused $750,000 in property damage and led to the loss of some 70 years of research; a July 2004 torching of a suburban lumberyard in Brigham, Utah, which caused $1.5 million in damage.

None of these attacks would have come close to qualifying for federal reinsurance under TRIA.

For a catalogue of these and other attacks linked to radical environmentalism, see Barcott, 2002; Stanton, 2001; Schabner, 2001a and b; "The Green Threat," 2001; and Knickerbocker, 2002.

aging and mitigating the financial risk of terrorist attacks in the United States, particularly in the event that a homegrown organization moves to execute a catastrophic act of political violence.

While the public policy justification is unclear for creating a distinction between the treatment of threats emanating from neo-Nazis in New Jersey and from transnational jihadists based in the Pakhtun tribal belt along the Pakistani-Afghan border, the practical application of this distinction may be difficult as well. Definitively distinguishing between strikes that are carried out at the behest of a foreign interest has become increasingly difficult given the fragmentation of the current al Qaeda structure. As noted in Chapter Three, the network now routinely relies on affiliates to carry out its assaults—especially citizens and/or established residents in targeted countries—many of whom act on their own initiative. If a U.S. national carries out a bombing on American soil, would this attack be considered a domestic act of aggression or one that is perpetrated at the behest of an external source? For example, had Jose Padilla actually executed his alleged dirty bomb plot in 2002, would it have been designated a certified act of terrorism (in which case it would have been covered by TRIA) or an independent action undertaken by a U.S. citizen reacting to the global appeal of transnational Islamist militancy (meaning that it would not)?

The example of the anthrax attacks in the United States in October 2001 provides another example of the complexity of this distinction. To date, the perpetrator of these attacks has not been identified, and it would not be possible to certify whether these attacks were of foreign or domestic origins. If these attacks occurred today and were large enough to trigger the invocation of TRIA, there is a potential to put some insurance companies at risk of insolvency but only if the attack was not certified. This confusion may hinder recovery from the attack.

CHAPTER FIVE

Conclusions

TRIA was intended to stimulate economic development by encouraging insurers to reenter the market and offer insurance that would cover a repeat of 9/11. The act has been moderately successful in achieving this goal by requiring that insurance for terrorist attacks perpetrated through conventional means by foreign terrorists be widely available. Additionally, such coverage costs have declined since 2002. In light of declining costs, the fraction of companies with commercial insurance that purchase terrorism coverage has increased since 2002 to about one-half.

This book has described the evolving terrorist threat, with the goal of comparing the underlying risk of attack to the architecture of financial protection that has been facilitated by TRIA. In this chapter, we outline the lessons learned for the renewal of TRIA in 2005, and for longer-term financial solutions to the risk of terrorism.

Key Lessons Learned

We have identified four key lessons learned, which we discuss below.

Conventional Attacks by Foreign Terrorists Against Commercial Targets Remain a Significant Risk in the United States

While some extraordinary successes have been achieved in the GWOT and in the protection of assets at risk in the United States, al Qaeda remains a significant threat. As long as this situation prevails, the need for financial tools to protect the private sector against large-scale terror attacks will remain.

Several Trends Have Converged to Shift Risks from the Public Sector Toward Private-Sector Assets Typically Covered by Insurance

The GWOT has changed the operational environment of al Qaeda and other terrorist groups, which has necessitated a shift in emphasis by terrorist groups to softer targets that are easier to attack and more likely to be in the private sector. This trend has been exacerbated by target hardening around prominent sites in the continental United States, which has triggered a process of threat displacement to easier-to-attack civilian-centric venues. Moreover, stimulated largely by the fiscal consequences of 9/11, bin Laden has increasingly cited the need to attack targets that will result in larger economic, cascading effects, which has further intensified the risk to the private sector. Finally, aside from al Qaeda, an increased focus on AG among groups that range from radical environmentalists to the far right has directly raised the risk to multinational corporate assets. Because all these trends point toward an increased focus on assets that are covered by insurance, they necessarily serve to reinforce the need for a functioning system of private-sector financial risk management for terrorism.

TRIA Has Significant Gaps and Is Not Robust to an Evolving Threat

This book has documented several significant gaps in the current system for terrorism insurance, some of which occur in areas that contemporary terrorism trends suggest will be risks in the future. In short, there is a real possibility of large uninsured losses accruing in the near-to-medium term, which will significantly impede the recovery from some future attacks. The most profound risk occurs in the area of CBRN attacks, for which insurers are not required to offer coverage (except under workers' compensation). The book discussed in particular the growing risk of a radiological attack, which could elicit sizable uninsured losses. Another significant gap is the exclusion of domestic attacks, which, while less of a risk than imported threats, nevertheless remain real and increasingly appear to be focusing on private-sector targets. The exclusion of domestic attacks is also problematic because it leads to confusion in light of the increased "franchising" of terrorist attacks by al Qaeda to local affiliates and the added difficulty of attributing attacks to a particular group. Finally, attacks on networks, such as airlines, trains, ports, and other critical infrastructure could lead to significant uninsured losses since costs associated with indirect damage loss are not typically covered by insurance.

TRIA Does Not Provide Adequate Financial Protection, Particularly in the Face of Economically Motivated Attacks

Specifically, take-up rates may be too low, increasing disruption after future attacks and undermining resilience. Discussions of TRIA have noted that take-up rates are equal to or higher than those for other kinds of catastrophic risks, such as hurricanes. These may be appropriate for natural disasters, but terrorism involves a national security dimension that this comparison obscures (Dixon and Reville, forthcoming). In particular, as al Qaeda increasingly advertises its interest in attacks with magnified economic consequences, it is increasingly important to fortify the institutions that buffer the economic consequences of such an attack. Insurance provides funds to compensate injured victims and the families of the deceased, to sustain business operations during disruption, and to rebuild damaged or destroyed assets and infrastructure. Take-up rates at current levels are likely to lead to widespread uninsured losses, which would slow recovery and magnify the economic consequences.

Policy Implications

The most prominent policy question about terrorism insurance is the renewal of TRIA. This book has noted that while the act has supported the growth of a market for terrorism insurance, the current system has significant gaps, is not robust to changes in the threat, and provides inadequate protection. To be sure, the focus of this study has been on the alignment between the risk and the threat, and many of the economic issues that have been prominent in the debates surrounding TRIA have not been addressed here.[1] That said, at least five observations can be extrapolated from the analysis that have relevance to terrorism insurance public policy in the United States.

TRIA's Sunset, Without Additional Congressional Action, Will Both Slow Recovery After a Future Attack and Magnify the Economic Consequences of an Attack, at Least in the Short Run

Since the government provides reinsurance under TRIA, its sunset is certain to raise the cost of terrorism insurance, which will lower take-up rates that are already arguably too low and increase the amount of uninsured losses following a future attack. The solvency of insurance companies may not be threatened if the companies manage their exposures to limit their risk, but this is precisely the activity that will raise the price and raise the risk of widespread uninsured losses.[2] Instead of allowing TRIA to sunset, particularly in the face of economically motivated terrorist attacks, Congress might prefer to consider policy measures that *increase* the take-up of insurance and *lower* its price.

A Long-Term Solution to Providing Terrorism Insurance in the United States Must Go Beyond the TRIA Framework

There is significant economic risk to the United States in uninsured losses resulting from CBRN attacks and attacks by domestic groups. Dropping the "foreign interest" designation for certified attacks under TRIA is a first step, but the CBRN problem is far more complicated, not the least because these attacks could lead to losses of enormous magnitude and coverage for them is not readily available. If an extension of TRIA included a mandatory offer of coverage for CBRN contingencies, the challenge for insurance companies in predicting

---

[1] The array of economic issues under the general category of the "insurability of terrorism" have not been addressed, including its predictability, the concentration of risk, the capacity of the industry, and other issues. See, for instance, Dixon et al., 2004; U.S. GAO, 2004; Kunreuther and Michel-Kerjan, 2004a; Congressional Budget Office, 2005; and Smetters, 2004.

[2] Workers' compensation insurers cannot limit their risk in this way, and insolvency of insurance companies writing workers' compensation insurance is a significant risk.

the consequences of CBRN attacks seems likely to be insurmountable for some time. In addition, several aspects of the current system, such as the $100 billion maximum and the omission of life insurance from TRIA would also be problematic. CBRN attack insurance may thus be an area where a direct government program, like War Risks Insurance, is appropriate.

The Role of Insurance in Protecting Critical Infrastructure Needs to Be Examined

Given the interdependent nature of America's critical infrastructure and the desire of al Qaeda to carry out attacks that lead to larger economic effects, the ability of insurance to buffer the effects of these losses and to restore the system after disruptions needs to be better understood. As Kunreuther and Michel-Kerjan point out, failures of a weak link in these complex, mutually dependent networks can have devastating effects on all parts of that system (Kunreuther and Michel-Kerjan, 2004b, p. 206). Mandatory requirements of adequate levels of insurance may be appropriate for companies owning or operating systems vital to the functioning of U.S. critical infrastructure (in which case it may also be appropriate for the cost of this insurance to be subsidized). Mandatory insurance for critical infrastructure would also serve to spread risk more broadly and thereby allow insurance companies to manage the risk more effectively. However, this solution requires further study because mandatory insurance raises complicated equity issues and would also require the identification of an insurer of last resort if insurance companies are unwilling to cover a particular facility.

The Ability of Insurance to Prompt Increased Security in the Private Sector Is Promising but Requires Further Research

Given the shift of risk toward the private sector, as documented in this book, the ability to use insurance as a vehicle to encourage increased security measures in the private sector requires additional investigation. Some have argued that TRIA, through its provision of free reinsurance, has actually disincentivized private security (Congressional Budget Office, 2005). However, further research is needed to verify this, since the decisions of private companies to purchase insurance and to adopt security measures are still poorly understood. Equally, there are complex issues involving interdependent security that may actually lead to too much private investment in security in the absence of government-supported insurance (Lakdawalla and Zanjani, forthcoming). Either way, a long-run solution to terrorism insurance should be designed to incorporate specific mechanisms, such as security-based premium discounts, so that appropriate security investments can be encouraged through private insurance. Because the private sector is likely to need assistance in evaluating the appropriateness of particular investments, these mechanisms will probably take the form of a public-private sector partnership model. Developing and refining these types of collaborative frameworks are priorities for further research.

Given the Dynamic Nature of the Terrorist Threat, TRIA or Its Replacement Should Be Designed to Be More Robust to Changes in the Underlying Risk

In the near term, a focused government-sponsored effort to design a robust and improved approach to ensuring the integrity of the private sector's system for risk management after terrorist attacks (a successor to TRIA) should be a priority in terrorism insurance legislation this year.[3] In the longer term, an oversight board could be established to systematically review TRIA or its successor's performance and ensure that the act's provisions remain relevant to evolving trends in terrorism.

---

[3] This was also suggested in Kunreuther and Michel-Kerjan, 2005. Specifically, they recommend a national commission on terrorism insurance.

Bibliography

Abernathy, Wayne, *Testimony Given Before the House Subcommittee on Capital Markets, Insurance and Government Sponsored Enterprises and the Subcommittee on Oversight and Investigations Committee on Financial Services,* Washington, D.C., April 27, 2004.

Abu Ghaith, Sulaiman, video aired on *al-Jazeera,* October 9, 2001.

"Alert Spurs 'Unprecedented' Steps," *CBSNews.com,* December 30, 2003. Online at http://www.cbsnews.com/stories/2003/12/31/terror/main590830.shtml (as of June 2005).

"Al-Jazirah Airs Al-Zawahiri Recording on 2nd Anniversary of 'Tora Bora Battle,'" *Al-Jazirah Satellite Channel Television,* in FBIS, December 19, 2003.

"Al-Qaeda Is Replicating, Rejuvenating and Reorganizing to Strike in the Region," *Straits Times* (Singapore), September 12, 2002.

"Al-Qaeda: Organization or Ideology? Interviews with Steven Simon, Jason Burke and Josh Meyer," *On Point,* November 25, 2003. Online at http://www.wbur.org (as of June 2005).

The Anarchist FAQ Editorial Collective: Iain McKay, Gary Elkin, Dave Neal, and Ed Boraas, *An Anarchist FAQ,* Version 11.1, January 10, 2005. Online at www.infoshop.org/faq/index.html (as of June 2005).

Anti-Defamation League, *The Quiet Retooling of the Militia Movement,* September 2004.

Anti-Defamation League, "Deceptive Web Site Attempts to Lure Anti-Globalization Activists to Neo-Nazi Movement," 2002. Online at http://www.adl.org/PresRele/Internet_75/4130_72.htm (as of June 2005).

"Anti-Globalization—A Spreading Phenomenon," *Perspectives,* Ottawa: Canadian Security Intelligence Service, Report Number 2000/08, August 22, 2000, pp. 1–3. Online at http://www.csis-scrs.gc.ca/eng/miscdocs/200008_e.html (as of June 2005).

Aon Corporation, *Terrorism Risk Management & Risk Transfer Market Overview,* New York: Aon Corporation, December 2004. Online at http://www.aon.com/about/publications/issues/2004_global_terrorism_wp.pdf (as of June 2004).

Applebome, Peter, "Radical Right's Fury Boiling Over," *New York Times,* April 23, 1995.

Bagli, Charles, "Tower's Insurance Must Pay Double," *New York Times,* December 7, 2004.

Barcott, Bruce, "From Tree Hugger to Terrorist," *New York Times,* April 7, 2002.

Beam, Louis, "Leaderless Resistance," *Seditionist,* February 1992. Online at http://www.louisbeam.com/leaderless.htm (as of June 2005).

"Bean There," *Economist,* January 11, 2003.

Bell, Jeff, "City Police Nab Accused Eco-Terrorist," *Times Colonist* (Canada), March 16, 2004.

Bergen, Peter, *Holy War Inc., Inside the Secret World of Osama bin Laden,* New York: The Free Press, 2002.

Biehl, Janet, and Peter Staudenmaier, *Ecofascism: Lessons for the German Experience,* Edinburgh: AK Press, 1995.

"Bioterror Plot," *ABC News,* January 9, 2003.

Blanche, Ed, "Arrests of Western Converts Indicates New Security Fears," *Jane's Intelligence Review,* February 2005, pp. 26–29.

Bodi, Faisal, "Al-Qaida Claims US Consulate Attack," *Aljazeera.net,* December 07, 2004. Online at http://english.aljazeera.net/NR/exeres/56F9EAA5-47FD-4378-BB06-44002192C7D3.htm (as of June 2005).

"Bomb Rocks UN Headquarters in Baghdad, *ABC News,* August 19, 2003.

Brown, Jeffery, et al., "An Empirical Analysis of the Economic Impact of Federal Terrorism Reinsurance," *Journal of Monetary Economics,* Vol. 51, July 2004, pp. 861–898.

Brown, Patricia, "Enabling and Disabling Ecoterrorists," *New York Times,* November 16, 2003.

Burke, Jason, "9/11 Two Years On," *Observer* (UK), September 7, 2003.

Campbell, Tanner, and Rohan Gunaratna, "Maritime Terrorism, Piracy and Crime," in Rohan Gunaratna, ed., *Terrorism in the Asia Pacific,* Singapore: Eastern Universities Press, 2003.

Carpenter, Betsey, "Redwood Radicals," *US News and World Report,* September 17, 1990.

Carus, Seth, *Bioterrorism and Biocrimes: The Illicit Use of Biological Agents in the 20th Century,* Washington D.C.: National Defense University, Center for Counterproliferation Research, July 1999.

Chalk, Peter, *Hitting America's Soft Underbelly: The Potential Threat of Deliberate Biological Attacks Against the U.S. Agricultural and Food Industry,* Santa Monica, Calif.: RAND Corporation, MG-135-OSD, 2004.

Chalk, Peter, "Grave New World," *Forum for Applied Research and Public Policy,* Spring 2000.

Chalk, Peter, *West European Terrorism and Counter-Terrorism: The Evolving Dynamic,* London: Macmillan Press, 1996.

Chen, David, "New Study Puts Sept. 11 Payout at $38 Billion," *New York Times,* November 9, 2004.

"Civil Aviation Post-9/11/01," 9-11 Research, 2005. Online at http://911research.wtc7.net/post911/aviation/civil.html (as of June 2005).

Clegg, Claude Andrew, *An Original Man: The Life and Times of Elijah Muhammad,* New York: St. Martin's Press, 1997.

Cockburn, Alexander, "An Open Door for Nuclear Terrorism," *Los Angeles Times,* July 3, 2003.

Cole, Juan, "Al Qaeda's Doomsday Document and Psychological Manipulation," paper presented at *Genocide and Terrorism: Probing the Mind of the Perpetrator,* Yale Center for Genocide Studies, New Haven, Conn., April 9, 2003.

Communauté Online, "Le CRIF denonce une alliance antisemite 'brun vert rouge,'" January 27, 2003. Online at http://www.lci.fr/news/0,,983050-VU5WX0lEIDUy,00.html (as of June 2005).

Congressional Budget Office, *Federal Terrorism Reinsurance: An Update,* Washington D.C.: Congress of the United States, January 2005.

Davidson-Smith, Tim, "Single Issue Terrorism," *CSIS Commentary,* No. 74, Ottawa: Canadian Security Intelligence Service, Winter 1998. Online at http://www.csis-scrs.gc.ca/eng/comment/com74_e.html (as of June 2005).

Degnan, John, "Oversight of the Terrorism Risk Insurance Program," written statement prepared for the Senate Committee on Banking, Housing, and Urban Affairs, May 18, 2004.

Department of Foreign Affairs and Trade (DFAT), *Global Issues Brief on the Economic Costs of Terrorism,* Canberra: DFAT Economic Analytical Unit, April 7, 2003.

"The Dirty Bomb Suspect: Lots of Questions, Few Answers," *Time,* June 11, 2002.

Dixon, Lloyd, John Arlington, Stephen J. Carroll, Darius Lakdawalla, Robert T. Reville, and David M. Adamson, *Issues and Options for Government Intervention in the Market for Terrorism Insurance,* Santa Monica, Calif.: RAND Corporation, OP-135-ICJ, 2004.

Dixon, Lloyd, and Robert T. Reville, "National Security and Compensation Policy for Terrorism Losses," in *Catastrophic Risks and Insurance: Policy Issues in Insurance No. 8,* Paris: Organization of Economic Cooperation and Development, forthcoming.

Dixon, Lloyd, and Rachel Kaganoff Stern, *Compensation for Losses from the 9/11 Attacks,* Santa Monica, Calif.: RAND Corporation, MG-264-ICJ, 2004.

"Does al-Qaida Have 20 Suitcase Nukes?" *WorldNetDaily.com*, October 2, 2002. Online at http://www.worldnetdaily.com/news/printer-friendly.asp?ARTICLE_ID=29109 (as of June 2005).

Doherty, Neil, Joan Lamm-Tennant, and Laura Starks, "Insuring September 11th: Market Recovery and Transparency," *Journal of Risk and Uncertainty,* Vol. 26, 2003.

Eagan, Sean, "From Spikes to Bombs: The Rise of Eco-Terrorism," *Studies in Conflict and Terrorism,* Vol. 19, 1996.

Earth Liberation Front (ELF), *Frequently Asked Questions About the Earth Liberation Front,* Portland, Oreg.: North American Earth Liberation Front Press Office, 2001.

Eccleston, Roy, "Bush Claims a Terror Scalp," *Australian,* March 3, 2003.

Eedle, Paul, "Terrorism.com," *Guardian* (London), July 17, 2002.

Ellis, John, "Terrorism in the Genomic Age," in Rohan Gunaratna, ed., *The Changing Face of Terrorism,* Singapore: Eastern Universities Press, 2004.

"Environmental Arson," *USA Today,* January 18, 1999.

Farley, Maggie, "In New York, U.N. Officials React with Agony, Resolve," *Los Angeles Times,* August 20, 2003.

Federal Bureau of Investigation (FBI), *Analysis of Protest Related Arrests,* Washington, D.C.: U.S. Department of Justice, 2001.

FBI, "Most Wanted Terrorists," undated. Online at http://www.fbi.gov/mostwant/terrorists/fugitives.htm (as of June 2005).

Finn, Peter, "Al Qaeda Deputies Harbored by Iran," *Washington Post,* August 28, 2002.

Flynn, Stephen, "The Neglected Homefront," *Foreign Affairs,* September/October 2004.

Freeh, Louis, Former Director of the FBI, *The Threat of Terrorism to the United States: Hearing Before the U.S. Senate, Committees on Appropriations, Armed Services and Select Committee on Intelligence,* May 10, 2001. Online at http://www.fbi.gov/congress/congress01/freeh051001.htm (as of June 2005).

"Full Transcript of bin Ladin's Speech," *Aljazeera.net,* November 1, 2004. Online at http://english.aljazeera.net/NR/exeres/79C6AF22-98FB-4A1C-B21F-2BC36E87F61F.htm (as of June 2005).

Furet, Francois, *The Passing of an Illusion: The Idea of Communism in the Twentieth Century,* Chicago and London: The University of Chicago Press, 1999.

Gold, Scott, "Case Yields Chilling Signs of Domestic Terror Plot," *Los Angeles Times,* January 7, 2004.

"The Green Threat," *Economist,* October 1, 2001.

Greenberg, Erice, "Right-Wing Militias Gain Troops After 9/11 Attacks," *Forward*, September 10, 2004.

Gunaratna, Rohan, "The al-Qaeda Threat and the International Response," in David Martin Jones, ed., *Globalisation and the New Terror,* Cheltenham, UK: Edward Elgar, 2004.

Gunaratna, Rohan, *Inside Al Qaeda: Global Network of Terror,* New York: Berkley Books, 2002.

Hartwig, Robert P., "The Cost of Terrorism: How Much Can We Afford," presentation to the National Association of Business Economics 46th Annual Meeting, Philadelphia, Pa., October 2004. Online at http://www.iii.org/media/presentations/tria/ (as of June 2005).

Hayden, H. Thomas, "Suitcase Nukes," *Military.com*, July 22, 2004. Online at http://www.military.com/NewContent/0,13190,Hayden_072204,00.html (as of June 2005).

Herbert-Burns, Rupert, "Terrorism in the Early 21st Century Maritime Domain," paper presented before the IDSS Maritime Security Conference, Singapore, May 20–21, 2004.

Hoffman, Bruce, "Al Qaeda, Trends in Terrorism and Future Possibilities: An Assessment," *Studies in Conflict and Terrorism,* Vol. 26, No. 6, December 2003.

Hoffman, Bruce, *Inside Terrorism,* London: Gollancz, 1999.

Hoffmann, Stanley, "Clash of Globalizations," *Foreign Affairs,* July/August 2002.

Home, Stewart, "Organized Chaos," *Independent* (UK), October 25, 1990.

Huband, Mark, Edward Alden, and Stephen Fidler, "The West Has Hit al-Qaeda Hard But Terrorism Is Still a Formidable Enemy," *Financial Times* (UK), September 11, 2003.

Hutchinson, Robert, "The Struggle for Control of Radioactive Sources," *Jane's Intelligence Review,* March 2003.

Hubbard, Glen, and Bruce Deal, *The Economic Effects of Federal Participation in Terrorism Risk*, study prepared by Analysis Group Inc., New York: Insurance Information Institute. September 14, 2004. Online at http://www.iii.org/media/latestud/TRIA/ (as of June 2005).

Islamic-World.Net, *Islamic-World's Thoughts on the War on Terrorism,* "Quote Section, Week 5," October 2001. Online at http://islamic-world.net/warnews/quote/week005.htm (as of June 2005).

"Italian Anarchists Probed in Letter-Bomb Campaign," *Globe and Mail* (Canada), December 31, 2004.

Jaffee, Dwight M., and Thomas Russell, "Behavioral Models of Insurance: The Case of the California Earthquake Authority," paper prepared for NBER Insurance Conference, 2000.

Jehl, Douglas, "Remotely Controlled Craft Part of U.S.-Pakistan Drive Against Al Qaeda, Ex-Officials Say," *New York Times,* May 16, 2005.

Jehl, Douglas, and David Johnston, "In Video Message, bin Laden Issues Warning to U.S.," *New York Times*, October 30, 2004.

Johnson, Kevin, and John Diamond, "Embassy Bombings Suspect Captured in Pakistan," *USA Today*, July 30, 2004.

Johnston, David, and Eric, Lichtblau, "Tourist Copters in New York City A Terror Target," *New York Times*, August 9, 2004.

"Journalist Says al-Qaeda Has Black Market Nuclear Bombs," *Sydney Morning Herald* (Australia), March 22, 2004.

Kenney, Michael, "From Pablo to Osama: Counter-Terrorism Lessons from the War on Drugs," *Survival,* Vol. 45, No. 3, Autumn 2003, pp. 187–206.

"Key Asian Terror Suspect Seized," *BBC News*, August 14, 2003. Online at http://news.bbc.co.uk/2/hi/americas/3152263.stm (as of June 2005).

King, Peter T., *Opening Statement Before the House Committee on Financial Services,* April 28, 2004.

Kingsworth, Paul, "The Global Backlash," *New Statesman,* April 28, 2003.

Kiser, Steve, *Financing Terror: Analysis and Simulation to Affect Al Qaeda's Financial Infrastructures,* dissertation, Santa Monica, Calif.: Pardee RAND Graduate School, RGSD-185, 2005.

Knickerbocker, Brad, "Ecoterrorists May Increase Ops in US," *Christian Science Monitor*, September 26, 2002.

Koch, Bernard (ed.), "Terrorism, Tort Law and Insurance: A Comparative Study," *Tort and Insurance Law Volume II,* New York: Springer-Verlag, 2004.

Kunreuther, Howard, and Erwann Michel-Kerjan, "Terrorism Insurance 2005: Where Do We Go from Here," *Regulation*, Spring 2005. Online at http://www.cato.org/pubs/regulation/index.html (as of June 2005).

Kunreuther, Howard, and Erwann Michel-Kerjan, *Insurability of (Mega)-Terrorism: Challenges and Perspectives,* Report to the OECD Task Force on Terrorism Insurance, Paris: Organization of Economic Cooperation and Development, December 2004a.

Kunreuther, Howard, and Erwann Michel-Kerjan, "Policy Watch: Challenges for Terrorism Risk Insurance in the United States," *Journal of Economic Perspectives,* Vol. 18, No. 4, Fall 2004b.

Kunreuther, Howard, Erwann Michel-Kerjan, and Beverly Porter, "Extending Catastrophe Modeling to Terrorism," in Patricia Grossi and Howard Kunreuther, eds., *Catastrophe Modeling: A New Approach to Managing Risk,* Boston, Mass.: Springer, 2005.

Kunreuther, Howard, Erwann Michel-Kerjan, and Beverly Porter, *Assessing, Managing and Financing Extreme Events: Dealing With Terrorism*, Cambridge, Mass.: National Bureau of Economic Research, Working Paper No. 10179, December 2003. Online at http://papers.nber.org/papers/w10179.

Lakdawalla, Darius, and George Zanjani, "Insurance, Self-Protection, and the Economics of Terrorism," *Journal of Public Economics,* forthcoming.

Lane, Charles, "Court Accepts Case of 'Dirty Bomb' Suspect," *Washington Post*, February 21, 2004.

Lee, Martha, "Violence and the Environment: The Case of 'Earth First!'" *Terrorism and Political Violence,* Vol. 7, No. 3, 1995.

"Letter Bombs Explode but Cause No Injuries," *Los Angeles Times,* January 6, 2004.

Lewis, Neil, "Judge Says U.S. Terror Suspect Can't Be Held As an Enemy Combatant," *New York Times*, March 1, 2005.

"A Limitless Risk," *Economist*, November 23, 2002.

MacFarquhar, Neil, "Saudis Support a Jihad in Iraq Not Back Home," *New York Times*, April 23, 2004.

Makarenko, Tamara, "Earth Liberation Front Increases Actions Across the USA," *Jane's Intelligence Review,* September 2003.

Manes, Christopher, *Green Rage: Radical Environmentalism and the Unmaking of Civilization,* Boston, Mass.: Little Brown and Company, 1990.

Marsh Inc., *Marketwatch: Property Terrorism Insurance Update—3rd Quarter 2004,* New York: Marsh and McLennan, December 2004.

"Maritime Security Measures," *Jane's Intelligence Review,* March 2003.

"Martyrdom and Murder—Suicide Terrorism," *Economist,* January 10, 2004.

Masood, Salman, and Mohammed Khan, "Pakistan Reports Arrest of Senior Qaeda Leader," *New York Times,* May 5, 2005.

McDonnell, Patrick, "US Defends Security Setup in Iraq," *Los Angeles Times,* March 4, 2004.

McGrory, Daniel, "French Tip Led Police to Poison Gang," *Australian,* January 10, 2003.

McKenzie, D., *National Economic Planning: Will It Fly?* Auburn, Ala.: Ludwig von Mises Institute, April 4, 2003. Online at http://www.goldeagle.com/gold_digest_03/mackenzie040403.html (as of June 2005).

Meyer, Josh, "Terrorists' Surveillance Effort May Be Broader," *Los Angeles Times,* August 8, 2004.

Michel-Kerjan, Erwann, "New Vulnerabilities in Critical Infrastructures: A U.S. Perspective," *Journal of Contingencies and Crisis Management,* Vol. 11, 2003.

Michel-Kerjan, Erwann, and Burkhard Pedell, "Terrorism Risk Coverage in the Post-9/11 Era: A Comparison of New Public-Private Partnerships in France, Germany and the U.S.," *The Geneva Papers on Risk and Insurance,* Special Issue 30th Anniversary, 2005.

Miller, Christian, "The Alleged Brains Behind bin Laden," *Los Angeles Times,* October 5, 2001.

"The Moment of Truth," *Economist,* May 17, 2003.

Nauess, Arne, "Deep Ecology and Ultimate Premises," *Ecologist,* 1998.

New Jersey Committee of Safety, "Global Governance: Does the United Nations Have a Plan for You?" Shamong, N.J., undated. Online at http://www.committee.org/NJcos/njcos06.htm (as of June 2005).

New Jersey Militia, Trenton, N.J. Online at http://www.njmilitia.org (as of June 2005).

"New Trends in Terrorism: Challenges for Intelligence and Counter-Terrorism," seminar, Lisbon, July 4–5, 2002.

"News Conference Regarding Zacarias Moussaoui," Washington, D.C.: Department of Justice Conference Center, December 11, 2001.

Nowotny, Walter, "Pro-White Nationalism Versus Globalization," *Pro-White Forum*, July 17, 2002. Online at http://www.churchoftrueisrael.com/nsforum/ns7-17.html (as of June 2005).

Office of the Coordinator for Counterterrorism, *Patterns of Global Terrorism, 2003*, Washington D.C.: United States Department of State, April 19, 2004.

Office of the Coordinator for Counterterrorism, *Patterns of Global Terrorism, 1998*, Washington D.C.: United States Department of State, April 1999.

"Officials: Dirty Bomb Plot Disrupted," *CNN News*, August 28, 2002.

Organization for Economic Cooperation and Development (OECD), *Report on Maritime Transport: Risk Factors and Economic Impact,* Paris: OECD, July 2003.

"The Other War," *Economist*, March 8, 2003.

Ottley, Ted, "Ted Kazcynski: The Unabomber," Crime Library.com, 2005. Online at http://www.crimelibrary.com/terrorists_spies/terrorists/kaczynski/1.html?sect=1 (as of June 2005).

Oxley, Mike, *Testimony Given Before the Subcommittee on Capital Markets, Insurance and Government Sponsored Enterprises,* Washington, D.C., April 28, 2004.

Pape, Robert, "The Strategic Logic of Suicide Terrorism," *American Political Science Review,* Vol. 97, No. 3, August 2003.

"P/C Terrorism Insurance Coverage: Where Do We Go Post–Terrorism Risk Insurance Act?" Washington, D.C.: American Academy of Actuaries Extreme Events Committee, May 2004.

"Person of the Week: Jose Padilla," *Time*, June 14, 2002. Online at http://www.time.com/time/pow/article/0,8599,262269,00.html (as of June 2005).

Peterson, Jonathan, and Josh Meyer, "Ridge Warns of Specific Threats," *Los Angeles Times*, August 2, 2004.

Philipkoski, Kristen, "Eco-Terror Cited as Top Threat," *Wired.com*, June 16, 2004. Online at http://www.wired.com/news/medtech/0,1286, 63812,00.html (as of June 2005).

Pierce, William, "Why Revolution?" in *The Best Attack! And National Vanguard Tabloid*, Hillsboro, W. Va.: National Vanguard Books, 1978.

Pitts, Joe, "Inequality Is No Myth," *Foreign Affairs*, July/August 2002.

Plante, Chris, "US Suspects al-Qa'ida in Morocco Bombings," *CNN News* May 18, 2003. Online at http://www.cnn.com/2003/WORLD/africa/ 05/17/al.qaeda.morocco/ (as of June 2005).

"Possible Plane Plot Against British Airways," *Command Post*, December 28, 2003. Online at http://www.command-post.org/gwot/2_archives/ 009253.html (as of June 2005).

"Post, Times Publish Unabomber Manifesto," *CNN News*, September 19, 1995. Online at http://www-cgi.cnn.com/US/9509/unabomber/ (as of June 2005).

RAND-MIPT Terrorism Incident Database. Online at http://www.tkb.org/ RandSummary.jsp (as of June 2005).

Ranstorp, Magnus, "Interpreting bin Laden's Fatwa," *Studies in Conflict and Terrorism*, Vol. 21, No. 4, October–December 1998.

Rashid, Ahmed, *The Taliban*, London: I.B. Tauris, 2000.

Resch, Kimberly, and Mathew Osborne, *WMD Terrorism and Usama bin Laden—Special Report*, Monterey, Calif.: Monterey Institute of International Studies, Center for Nonproliferation Studies, March 7, 2001. Online at http://cns.miis.edu/pubs/reports/binladen.htm (as of June 2005).

Ressa, Maria, "Fears of New Suicide Terrorism Squad," *CNN News*, February 26, 2004. Online at http://www.cnn.com/2003/WORLD/asiapcf/ southeast/08/11/alqaeda.blast/index.html (as of June 2005).

Richardson, Michael, *A Time Bomb for Global Trade*, Singapore: Institute for Southeast Asian Studies, 2004.

Riley, Mark, "Arsonists Sabotage Top Ski Resort," *Sydney Morning Herald*, October 24, 1998.

Roseboro, Brian, *Testimony Given Before the Senate Committee on Banking, Housing and Urban Affairs*, Washington, D.C., May 18, 2004.

Rosebraugh, Craig, "Contemplating Political Violence," *BJews.Com,* November 27, 2003. Online at http://www.bukharianjews.com/print.php?sid=62 (as of June 2005).

Rosebraugh, Craig, quoted on *Weekend All Things Considered,* National Public Radio, January 7, 2001.

Rubin, Alissa, "Iraq Seen as Terror Target," *Los Angeles Times*, August 10, 2003.

Ryan, Joan, "Not All Citizens Have Rights," *San Francisco Chronicle*, January 13, 2005.

"Saudi Bombing Deaths Rise," *BBC News*, May 13, 2003. Online at http://news.bbc.co.uk/1/hi/world/middle_east/3022473.stm (as of June 2005).

Savage, Charlie, "U.S. Sees Insurers As Possible Tool in Terror Fight, *Boston Globe,* February 22, 2005.

Schabner, Dean, "ELF Making Good on Threat," *abcNews.com*, January 30, 2001a.

Schabner, Dean, "Elusive Anarchists," *abcNews.com*, January 30, 2001b.

Schweitzer, Yoram, "The Ultimate Weapon?" *Review,* September 2001.

Shenon, Philip, "US Says Capture of Al Qaeda Leader May Provide Clues to Thwarting Terror Attacks," *New York Times*, November 23, 2002.

Shadow Financial Regulatory Committee, *A Proposed Federal Backstop for Terrorism Insurance and Reinsurance*, Washington D.C.: American Enterprise Institute, Statement No. 182, September 23, 2002. Online at http://www.aei.org/publications/pubID.14325,filter.all/pub_detail.asp (as of June 2005).

Shrader, Katherine, "Why No Suicide Bombers Here?" *Associated Press,* July 29, 2004. Online at http://www.zwire.com/site/news.cfm?BRD=1078&dept_id=151021&newsid=12534259&PAG=461&rfi=9 (as of June 2005).

Smetters, Kent, "Insuring Against Terrorism: The Policy Challenge," paper presented before the Conference of the Brookings-Wharton Papers on Financial Services, University of Pennsylvania, January 8–9, 2004. Online at http://irm.Wharton.upenn.edu/WP-Insuring-Smetters.pdf (as of June 2005).

Sprinzak, Ehud, "Rational Fanatics," *Foreign Policy,* September 2000.

Stanton, Sam, "Eco-Terrorism Group Claims Tulare Attack," *Sacramento Bee,* March 4, 2001.

Stiglitz, Joseph, *Globalization and Its Discontents,* New York: W.W. Norton, 2002.

Strauss, Mark, "Anti-Globalism's Jewish Problem," *Foreign Policy,* November/December 2003, pp. 61–65.

"Suicide Attack at U.S. Consulate in Pakistan Kills at Least 11," *Online NewsHour,* June 14, 2002. Online at http://www.pbs.org/newshour/updates/karachi_06-14-02.html (as of June 2005).

Sullivan, Robert, "The Face of Eco-Terrorism," *New York Times Magazine,* December 20, 1998.

"Suspects Allegedly Targeted South Africa," *Los Angeles Times,* August 5, 2004.

Tabor, James, and Eugene, Gallagher, *Why Waco? Cults and the Battle for Religious Freedom in America,* Berkeley, Calif.: University of California Press, 1995.

Taylor, Bron, "Religion, Violence and Radical Environmentalism: From Earth First! to the Unabomber to the Earth Liberation Front," *Terrorism and Political Violence,* Vol. 10, No. 4, Winter 1998.

Tenet, George, "The Worldwide Threat 2004: Challenges in a Changing Global Context," February 24, 2004. Online at http://www.cia.gov/cia/public_affairs/speeches/2004/dci_speech_02142004.html (as of June 2005).

"Terror Back in Business," *Australian,* May 15, 2003.

"Terrorists Blamed for Tanker Blast Off Yemen," *Financial Times* (London), October 8, 2002.

"Text of the World Islamic Front's Statement Urging Jihad Against Jews and Crusaders," *al-Quds al-Arabi* (London), February 23, 1998.

"Threats Ground Air France Flights," *CBSNews.com,* December 24, 2003, Online at http://www.cbsnews.com/stories/2003/12/24/terror/main590170.shtml (as of June 2005).

"A Timely Arrest," *Economist,* March 8, 2003.

Toffler, Alvin, "Will 'Green' Tide Create New Dark Age?" *Toronto Star* (Canada), November 27, 1990.

Towers Perrin, *Workers' Compensation Terrorism Reinsurance Pool Feasibility Study,* Stamford, Conn.: Towers Perrin, April 14, 2004. Online at http://www.towersperrin.com/tillinghast/publications/reports/WC_Terr_Pool/WC_Terr_Pool_Study.pdf (as of June 2005).

Tucker, David, "What Is New About Terrorism and How Dangerous Is It?" *Terrorism and Political Violence,* Vol. 13, No. 3, Autumn 2001.

"The Undead," *Economist,* May 24, 2003.

"U.S. Admits Rise in Terror Attacks," *BBC News,* June 22, 2004.

U.S. Congress, Terrorism Risk Insurance Act, 107 Congress, January 23, 2002, U.S.C. 101, 102, and 103.

U.S. Department of Homeland Security, *Threats & Protection,* "Advisory System: Homeland Security Advisory System," Washington, D.C. Online at http://www.dhs.gov/dhspublic/display?theme=29 (as of June 2005).

U.S. Department of the Treasury, *Terrorism Risk Insurance Testimony of the Honorable Paul H. O'Neill Secretary of the Treasury Before the Committee on Banking, Housing and Urban Affairs United States Senate,* Washington, D.C., October 30, 2001. Online at http://www.treas.gov/press/releases/po743.htm (as of June 2005).

U.S. Government Accountability Office (GAO), *Terrorism Insurance: Effects of the Terrorism Risk Insurance Act of 2003,* Washington, D.C.: GAO-04-806T, May 18, 2004.

Van Natta, Don, "Al Qaeda Hobbled by Latest Arrest, US Says," *New York Times,* March 3, 2003.

von Sternberg, Bob, "Call it Anarchism or New Left, It Has a Big Voice," *Star Tribune,* May 21, 2000.

Wald, Matthew, "Bill Allows Atomic Waste to Remain in Tanks," *New York Times,* October 10, 2004.

"Warning of More Attacks in Turkey," *CNN News,* November 20, 2003. Online at http://www.cnn.com/2003/WORLD/europe/11/20/turkey.blast/ (as of June 2005).

Weiner, Tim, "Focus on Arizona," *New York Times,* April 23, 1995.

Weiser, Benjamin, "Defense Grills Terror Witness on bin Laden," *New York Times*, February 14, 2001a.

Weiser, Benjamin, "Witness Describes Break with Group Led by bin Laden," *New York Times*, February 8, 2001b.

"Who Dunnit?" *Economist, October* 12, 2002.

"Who Is Richard Reid," *BBC News*, December 28, 2001. Online at http://news.bbc.co.uk/1/hi/uk/1731568.stm (as of June 2005).

"Why An Appeals Court Opinion on Jose Padilla is Not Anti-Government," *CNN News*, January 28, 2004. Online at http://www.cnn.com/2004/LAW/01/28/findlaw.analysis.lazarus.padilla/ (as of June 2005).

Willan, Philip, "Anarchists Pose Biggest Threat to Italian National Security," *Jane's Intelligence Review,* December 2004, pp. 18–20.

Williams, Daniel, "At Least 20 Dead in Baghdad Blast," *Washington Post*, January 19, 2004.

Wilson, Peter, "Train Sabotage 'Retaliation' for Waco Shoot-Out," *Australian*, October 11, 1995.

Wright, Lawrence, "The Man Behind bin Laden," *New Yorker,* September 16, 2002.